DA CAPO PRESS SERIES IN
ARCHITECTURE AND DECORATIVE ART
General Editor: ADOLF K. PLACZEK
Avery Librarian, Columbia University

Volume 36

SELECT ARCHITECTURE

SELECT ARCHITECTURE

Being Regular Designs of Plans and Elevations
Well Suited to both Town and Country

By Robert Morris

New Foreword by Adolf K. Placzek
Avery Librarian, Columbia University

DA CAPO PRESS • NEW YORK • 1973

Library of Congress Cataloging in Publication Data

Morris, Robert, 1701-1754.
    Select architecture.

    (Da Capo Press series in architecture and decorative
art, v. 36)
    Reprint of the 1757 ed.
    1. Architecture—Early works to 1800. 2. Archi-
tecture—Designs and plans. I. Title.
NA997.M67A55   1973   720′.942   72-87427
ISBN 0-306-71573-2

This Da Capo Press edition of *Select Architecture*
is an unabridged republication of the second edition
published in London in 1757. The new foreword has
been prepared especially for this reprint.

FOREWORD

In the glamourous galaxy of eighteenth-century architects, Robert Morris appears to be a faint star, sometimes almost invisible, sometimes obscured by the more conspicuous luminaries of his constellation, sometimes simply overlooked. An important star he is, nonetheless.

Why obscured? First of all, Robert Morris had the bad luck to be confused perpetually with his "kinsman" (as he called him) and mentor, Roger Morris, a well-connected and active architect who lived from 1695 to 1749. It was Roger who built the famous Palladian bridge at Wilton, one of England's most charming structures, for the Earl of Pembroke. It was Roger—not Robert—whose work is illustrated in Colin Campbell's *Vitruvius Britannicus,* that first great record of English classical architecture. On the other hand, little is known of Robert's life and of his work as an architect. Indeed, his birth and death dates have only recently been discovered (by John Fleming) through a hand-written note in one of Morris' books in the Royal Institute of British Architects Library: according to that note, Morris was born in 1701 and died in 1754. He is known to have done some architectural work in 1740 and in 1753. He may—or he may not—have completed Inveraray Castle in the Scottish Highlands for the Duke of Argyll after Roger's death. He may—or he may not—have executed some minor commissions. But he did without doubt write several important books, and it is his books, not his buildings, which make him a star of assured magnitude, a magnitude likely to become more apparent with our increasing knowledge of eighteenth-century England.

The phase in English architecture represented by Robert Morris—and by Roger as well—has been given many names. It has been called Early Georgian, after its historical framework, or even Whig, after its political base; Palladian, after its Italian Renaissance paragon, Andrea Palladio (1508–1580), or Burlingtonian, after Richard Boyle, third Earl of Burlington (1694–1753), the powerful, determined, doctrinaire, and probably brilliant leader of the group which came to dominate English architectural taste and design almost totally between 1720 and 1750. Nor has there been any general agreement on whether to call this Burlingtonian Palladianism a style, a school, or a movement. Morris himself speaks of the "Palladian manner."

The Palladians came into prominence partly as a reaction against the freer and more imaginative interpretation of Renaissance forms which can be called the English Baroque—a Baroque very different from the exuberant creations of the South Germans and Austrians and from the complex spatial compositions of Bernini and Borromini, a restrained, indeed an *English* sort of Baroque, based in part on French and Flemish antecedents. For all its comparative restraint, however, this Baroque was a great style, and some of England's greatest architects were its protagonists: Christopher Wren, Nicholas Hawksmoor, John Vanbrugh, James Gibbs. Palladianism succeeded this style, coming to more or less official power in 1718 with the ungracious dismissal of the eighty-six-year-old Wren from the office of Surveyor-General and his replacement by a Burlingtonian strawman. The Burlingtonians produced no architects of comparable imaginative power. They produced, instead, a school—bookish, academic, and in wonderful taste. Besides Burlington himself, there were Colin Campbell, William Kent, Isaac Ware, Henry Flitcroft, the already mentioned "kinsman" Roger Morris and some quite minor characters. Still, many delightful buildings, and some great ones, were designed—Burlington's own Chiswick, Campbell's Houghton Hall and Mereworth Castle, and Kent's Holkham Hall, among others. As these examples suggest, the emphasis was on country houses; it was among the great nobles that Palladianism held sway.

Stated in simple terms, the Burlingtonian tenet was that there is a correct way to build, and therefore an incorrect one. The correct way was, of course, the Roman way, as adapted in the sixteenth century by Andrea Palladio. Palladio had had a definite attraction for the English mind long before Burlington. It was actually Inigo Jones (1573–1652), the pioneer of the Italian Renaissance style in England, who discovered him for the English, and the Burlingtonians held Jones in high esteem—Morris, in fact, called him the British Palladio. This remark is significant not only for showing the character of Morris' highest praise but also for illustrating another aspect of the Burlingtonians—their new nationalism. By denying contemporary continental influences, mainly French, in favor of sixteenth-century and Roman ones—that is, far-away models—they could arrive at a mode of expression of their own, a sensible, sensitive, rational, and powerful Englishness behind a mask of antiquity. This nationalism is even more evident in Burlingtonian landscape design. Here the trend was all towards the naturalness ("naturalizing") of the garden, as practiced by William Kent and the famous "Capability" Brown. At first sight, this would seem a contradiction, since the trend in architecture was so strongly toward formality; but when viewed partly as a reaction against the French garden, the English garden of the English Palladians becomes historically understandable.

A series of great publications was part of the Palladian movement—they were, to repeat, a bookish lot. Above all, there is the great illustrated survey of English classic architecture, Colin Campbell's *Vitruvius Britannicus* (3 vols., 1715–1725). There are two translations of Palladio's basic *Quattro libri dell'architettura,* that bible of the English Palladians, one by Giacomo Leoni, the other by Isaac Ware. There is William Kent's *Designs of Inigo Jones* (1727). There are elaborate books on Roman thermae and Roman villas produced under the auspices of Lord Burlington. But noteworthy, indeed revealing, is the lack of any theoretical writing. Burlington himself did not write a word about architecture. Campbell, Kent, and Ware did not develop or disseminate any abstract theory—nor, for that matter, did their master, Inigo Jones. Purity of design, correctness, practicality, grandeur—all these things counted; but the complex thought behind them was never expressed. Again, one is tempted to say that this was a peculiarly English bent, especially when compared with the richness of Italian and French theoretical writing.

It is at this point that Robert Morris' star begins to shine, for he appears as the only theoretical writer of the Burlingtonian-Palladian movement. This does not mean that he is only, or merely, a theoretician. The designs which form the body of his books are charming, as can be seen from the plates which follow, and they are frequently quite original. But the theoretical inclination does set him apart from the better-known members of his group—even from his actively building but silent kinsman, Roger.

Robert Morris published several books and contributed engravings to others. There is, first of all, his *Essay in Defence of Ancient Architecture; or, a Parallel of the Ancient Buildings with the Modern: shewing the Beauty and Harmony of the Former, and the Irregularity of the Latter...To which is Annexed, an inspectional Table, universally Useful* (1728). I have quoted this title at length because it conveys all the elements of Palladianism: an unbounded admiration for Roman architecture, a desire to read into it rules of proportions which cannot be measured with certainty, and a critical attitude toward Baroque aberrants from the true norm.

Morris' next book, *Lectures on Architecture, Consisting of Rules Founded upon Harmonick and Arithmetical Proportions in Buildings...* (1734-36), goes even further. In order to give these lectures, he founded a group which he solemnly called The Society Established for the Improvement of Arts and Sciences. The lectures, as the title indicates, develop a system of proportions (based on cubic units) applicable to everything from a great villa to a chimney. The result would seem like an exercise in pendantry were it not lightened by the author's elegant style, good humor, and eighteenth-century liberalism ("design'd as an agreeable entertainment for gentlemen..."). It is, however, Palladianism at its strictest, to the point even of occasionally rapping Palladio's knuckles for not being Palladian enough. Symmetry, regularity, proportions rule supreme—except, of course, in landscape design, where Nature (with a capital N) takes over. Gothicism is detested, although several Palladians (above all, Kent) had a flirtation with the Gothic revival and Morris himself is reputed to have completed Inveraray Castle, one of the earliest of the Neo-Gothic follies.

We now come to one of the high points of Morris' achievements, his *Select Architecture*. There are some odd things about this book: first of all, it was published in 1755, a year after the author's death. Therefore, it is not certain whether the title *Select Architecture* was assigned by Morris himself or by Robert Sayer, the enterprising bookseller-printer of Fleet Street. (The second edition, reproduced in the following pages, came out only two years later, indicating a considerable success.) Furthermore, Morris had published the identical plates and the identical introduction in 1750 under the more modest but also somewhat misleading title, *Rural Residences,* a volume which, however, included a list of subscribers not present in either edition of *Select Architecture*. Otherwise, even the title vignette is the same, a design of which Robert Morris was fond and which appears in several of his works as an illustration of his theory of cubic proportions—in this case double cubes with circumscribing circles.

It will be evident immediately that *Select Architecture* was not meant to be a handbook for builders and artisans like the numerous works of William Halfpenny and Batty Langley. It was a book for lovers of architecture—and for clients of architects. It was also a book with a definite point of view. The introduction is a noteworthy brief explanation of Morris' architectural theory, historical approach,

FOREWORD

and aesthetics. The explanations to the plates are highly instructive and, like the introduction, contain a certain amount of theory. As a quite unusual feature, they also list prices, ranging from twenty-four pounds for a garden seat (plate 4) to 16,400 pounds for a villa (plate 22). Apart from this grand villa, Morris deals with the medium range, which undoubtedly was one of the reasons why the book was so popular in the American colonies. The plates show relatively modest structures, at last applying to such structures the Palladian-Burlingtonian taste that had long been indifferent to them. Morris, it might be said, takes Palladianism from Colin Campbell's high aristocratic seats to the middle class—to the town house (plate 1), the market place (plate 34), the village church (plate 45), and even to the farm (plate 33). Since this broadened the range of the movement to encompass the totality of English life, it can be said that in *Select Architecture*, Palladianism showed itself at last as a style rather than a taste.

The designs of the fifty plates are of unusual consistency. The stress—in the words of the introduction—is on simplicity, plainness, neatness, and "just proportion" (a matter of great concern to Morris). What emerges—in theory as well as in design—is a combination of traditionalism and rationalism, of "plainness" and sophistication.

Select Architecture appeared at a time when Palladianism was already on the wane. Lord Burlington had died in 1753, Kent in 1748, Campbell as early as 1729. New forces—Neo-Classicism, Romanticism, the Gothic Revival—were on the rise. New names—Robert Adam, William Chambers, and later John Soane—were coming on the scene. Nevertheless, *Select Architecture* remained a popular and influential book. Its anti-Rococo tenor and its emphasis on pure geometric forms appealed to the Neo-Classicists who were to be the taste-makers of the next generation. Robert Adam was a friend of Morris' and certainly knew his works. In America, the book —for reasons already mentioned—had a particular effect. We know that Thomas Jefferson owned and used it; we can even surmise that the octagon room in Monticello had its origin in plates 30 and 47. Peter Harrison, of Newport fame, is also recorded as having owned *Select Architecture,* and its influence can be seen in many American designs of the eighteenth-century. In recent times, it has become almost unobtainable. It is good to have this important and delightful book available again.

March 1970   Adolf K. Placzek
Avery Library

SELECT ARCHITECTURE

S E L E C T
ARCHITECTURE:
BEING
REGULAR DESIGNS
OF
PLANS and ELEVATIONS

Well fuited to both TOWN and COUNTRY;

IN WHICH

The Magnificence and Beauty, the Purity and Simplicity of DESIGNING,
For every Species of that noble Art,
Is accurately treated, and with great Variety exemplified,
From the Plain TOWN-HOUSE to the Stately HOTEL;
And in the Country from the genteel and convenient FARM-HOUSE
to the PAROCHIAL CHURCH.

With Suitable Embellifhments.
A L S O

BRIDGES, BATHS, SUMMER-HOUSES, &c. with ESTIMATES to each DESIGN by the
GREAT SQUARE, and fuch REMARKS, EXPLANATIONS and SCALES are annexed,
that the Comprehenfion is rendered eafy, and Subjeᴄt moft agreeable.

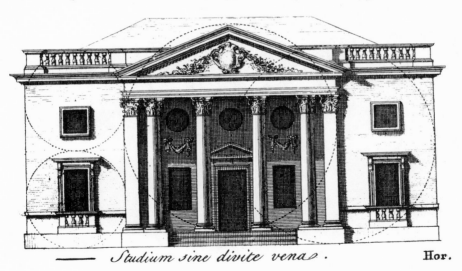

—— *Studium sine divite vena* .   Hor.

Illuſtrated with FIFTY COPPER PLATES, *Quarto.*
By *ROBERT MORRIS*, Surveyor.
The SECOND EDITION.

L O N D O N:
Sold by ROBERT SAYER, oppofite Fetter-Lane, in Fleet-Street.   MDCCLVII.
Price bound 13*s.*

PREFACE.

*S*OME *Years since, I began a Work something analogous to This: I had divided it into Two Parts; the First consisted of* Plans *and* Elevations, *for* Town-Houses; *the Second, for Buildings of various* Constructions *for the* Country: *And I had carried it so far into Execution, as to compleat the* Drawings.——*Something interfered that prevented my Intention; and it lay dormant till about a Year past.*——*I then examined what I had before undertaken, and flattered myself, that by a careful Revisal, I might meet with Encouragement, to compleat an Essay of this Kind, wholly adapted to the Uses of the* Country, *and to drop my Purpose of treating upon* Town-Houses.

Two or three Motives induced me to it: The First was, that there are already published, *and* executed, *such a Variety of* Town-Houses, *and so many Persons who are daily concerned in the* practical *Part of that Branch, that I was doubtful how it might be received.*—— *I thought,* Variety *and* Novelty *(the present reigning* Taste*) might be wanting to support it, which intimidated me from the Pursuit of it.*

The Second was, that to so few Persons, residing in the Country, *that are capable of* Designing, *something of this Nature might be acceptable, I hoped, at least, for Success to it: And I have earnestly endeavoured to render it useful in the* Appropriation, *and intelligible to every Capacity.*

Another was, That most who have wrote on this Subject, have raised nothing but Palaces, *glaring in* Decoration *and* Dress; *while the* Cottage, *or plain little* Villa, *are passed by unregarded.*——Gaiety, Magnificence, *the rude* Gothic, *or the* Chinese *unmeaning Stile, are the Study of our modern Architects; while* Grecian *and* Roman Purity *and* Simplicity, *are neglected.*

As an Admirer of those last *mentioned, I place myself, and my following* Designs, *before you. I have chose to copy the harmonious Dictates which* Nature *and* Science *teach; preferring* Plainness *and* Utility, *to* Gaiety *and* Ornament; *those I leave to their Votaries: If I have any where attempted to introduce them, it was merely to shew where they might be placed; and there I have been always very sparing.*

I think a Building, well proportioned, without Dress, *will ever please; as a plain Coat may fit as graceful, and easy, on a* well-proportioned *Man; —it will not alter the Agreeableness of either: But if you will be lavish in* Ornament, *your* Structure *will look rather like a* Fop, *with a Superfluity of gaudy* Tinsel, *than a* real Decoration.

There

PREFACE.

There are some few Things, in the Prosecution of this Undertaking, which may be necessary for me to explain.——I have not figured the Magnitude of any Room, the Thickness of any Wall, the Height or Breadth of any Door or Window, Dress or Ornament whatever : —— If I had, such Figuring, in so small Drawings, would make the Plans unintelligible : And to supply that seeming Defect, I have, to each Design, annexed a Scale of Feet, whereby a Knowledge of those Things may be easily obtained by a Pair of Dividers ; and if the Use of a Scale is not known by a Reader, the general Construction of the Whole will be very little understood by them ; and for such as do, they will be the better able to calculate the Parts, and see farther into the Uses and Convenience of the whole Building.

In the next Place, as most of these Designs are drawn to a small Scale, I have not introduced an Ionic or Corinthian Cornice : According to the Propriety of the Order, I thought it necessary, if I kept only strict to the general Proportion ; nor am I solicitous in these, or such minute Drawings, to have a Modilion, or Dentel, or either ; for it must be, in this Case, understood, that the Reader, as well as myself, knows the particular Members ; for which Reason, I did not think it absolutely necessary, to be at the Trouble to delineate them.

Another Thing may be imputed to Neglect : I have not set down the Uses and Distribution of the Apartments of any Structure ; because every different Room may be, by every new Inhabitant, converted to a different Use, so that what an Architect may design for a Parlour, may, by another, be metamorphosed into a Bedchamber ; a Stable I have known changed into a Kitchen ; and many other Apartments to have underwent as many Transmutations as are represented in Ovid.

I hope minute Improprieties will not be imputed to an indolent Neglect ; if, in general, I have given such Ideas of my Intention as are intelligible, let Half of what is wanting be supposed owing to a close Attention to other Business, and I will voluntarily take Censure on myself for the other Half.

Some few Errors in the Engraving, may have escaped my Notice, but I believe they are of such a Nature, that they are pardonable. My general Design, has been to introduce Convenience, Proportion and Regularity, with as much Variety as an Essay of this Kind would admit.

I have now, in this Preface, said what I thought necessary relating to myself ; and to give some Idea of the following Designs, I shall, as a proper Introduction to the Work, attempt some Remarks and Observations, which may be conducive to illustrate the Subject, and to render it both instructive and entertaining, and in which the Beauty and Simplicity of Designing, shall be more particularly considered by

ROBERT MORRIS.

INTRODUCTION.

THE *Science* I am treating on, is made univerfal through Neceffity : It fprung from Diftrefs, and Utility was the View of the Defigner. In the firft Ages of the World, its Extent was from the *Torrid* to the *Frigid Zone.* In the burning Sands of *Lybia*, and *Greenland's* icy Banks, its Veftigia may be traced; and in every Structure, in every Climate, Nature has dictated the Architect to the Difpofal of it, for Ufe and *Convenience :* Drefs and Decoration, were the Refinements of a long Series of Ages, the Improvements of *Greece,* and afterwards the Source of *Roman* Greatnefs.

Vitruvius, in his firft Chapter, Book II. fays, Men, in primitive Times, were born in Woods, or Caverns of the Earth, like the *Brute Creation* ; and with them had one favage Nutriment. Neceffity led them into a natural Affociation: They affembled by Signs ; and by different Sounds from their Mouths, they found they fignified certain Things ; from thence with Difficulty they formed Words and Speech.

Thus affembling and converfing together, mutual Wants, mutual Interefts and Prefervation, led them to dwell in the fame Place. They had different Difpofitions of Mind, that Nature had not given to other *Animals*, capable of forming an Idea of what was beautiful and magnificent in the Univerfe; and of performing with their Hands and Fingers, what the Reft of animated Beings were deprived of. They were naturally docile, and fufceptible of Imitation: The Inclemencies of the *Climes* and *Seafons,* led them, in each, to preferve Warmth in the colder Regions, and Coolnefs in the more intemperate Heat.

They began to erect their Dwellings with Branches of Trees, and with Mofs and Turf; they inclofed the Work with Leaves of Trees, and Reeds on them: They covered the Turf to defend themfelves from the Sun and Rain; but by Experience they found this Covering was not fufficient againft the Inclemency of the Winter : They raifed the Roofs proportioned to the Climate, that the Snow, or Rain, might cafily flide off, and not penetrate through the lower Covering.

The firft Buildings were made in this Manner ; and it is eafy to judge by thofe we fee now, that the Manner and fame Materials are ufed in *France* and *Spain*, and in *Aquitain*, their Houfes are covered with Turf (this was in the Time of *Vitruvius*; and he farther fays) in the Kingdom of *Chalchis*, there is found vaft Quantity of Wood. They made their Plan a Circle ; their Rafters were Boughs of Trees, which they placed

equidiftant

equidiftant at Foot, meeting in one Point at Top ; thefe they cover with Mofs and Turf ; and with Reeds, or fuch fmooth Covering, they finifh the Out-fide : Others made their Plan fquare, and in that Form high enough to ftand upright without being incommoded ; and on that fquare Part they placed a Roof, and covered it in the fame Manner.

The *Phrygians*, which inhabited a Country where there were no Forefts to furnifh them with Wood to build, found little Hillocks naturally raifed ; to thefe they made a Path to enter into it at the Foot of the Hillock, and as large as the Place would admit ; over this they put fmall Pieces of Wood, covered them with Reeds and Loom, and on this, when dry, they raifed a Mount of Earth, covering it with Turf : This made their Habitations warm in Winter, and cool in Summer ; and as Countries and Climates differ in Temperature, and Produce of Materials, Nature points out a Path in each for Defence againft the Inclemencies of Seafons, and other Self-Prefervation. From all which *Vitruvius* concludes, it is fufficient to judge, what have been the Buildings of the Antients.

I muft obferve here, that an Idea may be eafily formed of what *Vitruvius* afferts, if we compare with them thoufands of *Mudwall*, and *Thatched* Buildings. In *England* and *Wales*, we fee *Huts* and *Cottages* built in the fame Manner, juft as if the Inhabitants had newly ftarted into Being, and were led by *Nature* and *Neceſſity*, to form a Fabric, for their own Prefervation, from the Inclemencies of the Seafon, or other more prevalent Motive. I have feen many, whofe Afpect and Compofition are as fimple and mean, as thofe defcribed by *Vitruvius*.

He obferves, that as Nature has furnifhed us with all Sorts of Materials, they are only cultivated by the Practice of the Art of Building ; that they are brought to high Perfection with the Help of other Arts, which include the Neceffity of *Ornament* and *Decoration* for the Delicacies of Life ; and in which this Essay on the Primitive State of Building will naturally lead me to confider the *Convenience*, *Proportion*, and *Regularity*, as well as the Purity and Simplicity of Defigning.

Every *Cave* and *Hut* was made to anfwer fome End, and fuch Structure would be every where alike convenient, were the Climate and the Inhabitant alike circumftanced ; but Encreafe of Families encreafed the Wants and enlarged the Boundaries : From the Hut arofe the Cottage ; the Plots they cultivated were extended, and new Interefts rendered it neceffary to form Societies, to make Laws, &c. by which they fubjected themfelves to be governed. The wifeft and beft who formed them, were chofe to direct and rule their little States in their Infancy. Their Dwellings were enlarged for them, and their Attendants, and from thence arofe new Extenfions, new Wants of Convenience, &c. as the Nature of the Inhabitant, Law-giver, or Dependents required.

Convenience,

Convenience, *in this Light,* was not all : Another Sort, perhaps the moſt neceſſary, was, proper Choice of Situation. Wiſely they conſulted *Nature*; none willingly expoſed their Habitations to *bleak* and *tempeſtuous* Winds ; to the Inclemency of the Seaſons without natural or acquired *Shelter* and *Shade*; and with this was placed the eaſily attainable Neceſſaries to ſubſiſt on. *Food, Fuel* and *Water,* were abſolutely convenient, and Things of the higheſt Importance in Life; without either, Man would be incapable of preſerving himſelf or Domeſticks: They are the chief Ingredients to accommodate ſocial Beings. Raiment might, perhaps, with more Facility be obtained; but without theſe, the Chain that holds together Societies would be broke.

Vitruvius, in the Preface to his ſecond Book, tells us, that " *Dinocrates,* a Great Genius, went in Diſguiſe, where *Alexander* was ſitting on his Throne to diſtribute Juſtice, *(his Dreſs was a Lion's Skin thrown over him like a Mantle, &c. which is particularly deſcribed by* Vitruvius.) The Novelty of the Figure he made, ſurprized *Alexander*; who demanded what he was ? He anſwered, I am the *Macedonian Architect,* Dinocrates. I have brought *Alexander* Ideas and Deſigns worthy his Dignity ; I have made *Mount Athos* in the Form of a Man, who holds in his Left-Hand, a great City; in his Right, a Baſon which receives the Waters of *all* the *Rivers* that fall from this *Mountain* to the *Sea*."

" *Alexander,* pleaſed with the Invention, aſked him, if he had any Country round this *City* to ſupply it with *Fuel, Herbage,* or other Nutriment, to ſubſiſt the Inhabitants; and finding there could be none, but muſt be brought ſome Diſtance by Sea, he told *Dinocrates,* I approve the *Beauty* and *Magnificence* of your Deſign ; but to eſtabliſh a Colony in the Place you propoſe muſt be impracticable; and though I commend its *Grandeur,* I muſt diſlike the Place you have choſen to execute it in."

" Some Time after, *Alexander* diſcovered a *Port,* which had a fine Harbour, an Acceſs to it eaſy, environed with a fertile Country, and which had the fineſt of all the Productions of the great River *Nilus.* Here he commanded *Dinocrates* to build a City, and which he called, after his own Name, Alexandria."

I have tranſlated this Paſſage, to ſhew, that proper Choice of Situation, from a City to a Cottage, will be in Proportion to the *Wants* and *Conveniences* required in either : In both, *Water, Fuel, Food,* &c. the great Ingredients neceſſary for Society, muſt be eaſily obtained, and alſo the Plenty and Value ſhould be regarded.

Convenience thus conſidered, in Point of the Diſpoſition of the Apartments, and a juſt Appropriation to the Wants and Uſes required, and alſo a proper Situation whereon to erect the Fabric, and where every

neceſſary

neceſſary Suſtenance is circumſtanced, as I obſerved; the next Point in view will be PROPORTION; and this muſt alſo be underſtood in two Lights.

The firſt is, the *natural Proportion* to adjuſt and diſpoſe the Plan to the Uſe of the Inhabitants, not to croud the Apartments with a numerous Throng, nor make ſo much Room for the Attendants, as not to be within Sight or Call, of their ſeveral reſpective Attendances; both which Extreams are carefully to be avoided. Uſeleſs and empty Rooms are ſo many additional Incumbrances in a Structure, and equally blameable as having too little, and in all which they are to be proportioned to the Dignity of the principal Inhabitant. The Parts ſhould be ſo diſpoſed, that, from the higheſt Station, in thoſe little Communities, all the ſubſervient Apartments ſhould be joined by an eaſy Gradation, that every Link in the Concatenation ſhould be juſtly regulated; and in this Light I would be underſtood, that they could no where elſe be ſo well placed. As in Hiſtory Painting, one principal Figure poſſeſſeth the ſuperior Light, the fore Ground and Eminence of the Piece, and the ſubordinate Figures are placed Part in Sight, Part in Groups and Shade for Contraſt, and keeping in the Deſign; ſo in Building, all the ſubſervient Offices ſhould terminate by gradual Progreſſion in *Utility* and *Situation*.

The other *ſimple Proportion*, is with Regard to *Geometrical* and *Harmonic* Magnitude; and theſe reſpect chiefly, *Beauty*, well regulated: There are certain Proportions in Building which affect the Mind through the Eye, as well as Muſic does through the Ear, and the injudicious in both will (in juſt Proportion) tell you they are pleaſed; but perhaps can aſſign no Reaſon why they are. The Cauſes are equal in both: A Jarring and Diſcord in Muſic immediately offends the *Ear*; a diſproportionate Building diſpleaſes the Eye: Proportion in *Tone* and *Magnitude* are the Cauſe. In my *Lectures* on *Architecture*, publiſhed in 1736, on the *Harmonic* and *Arithmetical* Proportions in Building, I ſaid all I then thought neceſſary on them, and to which at preſent I have nothing farther to add.

REGULARITY is the next eſſential Ingredient neceſſary in Building: Uniformity of Parts juſtly proportioned, and appropriated, will, as I obſerved before, ſtrike or affect the Mind, and this ariſes from a proper Arrangement of the ſeparate Diviſions in the Fabric, which, as in Muſic, compoſe the whole: One Part ſhould fit and anſwer to another, as Notes and Tones in Muſic, otherwiſe Diſcord will enſue; the different Parts muſt anſwer in Dreſs and Proportion; a Sameneſs of Ornament, or Plainneſs ſhould run through the Range, and be adapted to the Uſes of the Fabric or the Dignity of the Inhabitant; but even in *this*, Profuſeneſs of Ornament, eſpecially *external*, is carefully to be avoided. Time ſoon

feeds

feeds upon Dainties of that Kind; Feftoons of Fruits and Flowers are his delicious Repaft. The once magnificent Fabrics of Marble, *Greece* and *Rome*, have been TIME's Banquet ; they foon felt the deftructive Wafte, and even the more *plain* and *fimple* Ornaments are long fince crumbled into Duft.

In the preceding general Obfervations, I have, as concifely as I could, fhewn in what the *Convenience*, *Proportion*, and *Regularity* of the Structure confifts, and though no abfolute ftated Rules can be afcertained ; yet, in general, it may give fuch an Idea of the Ufefulnefs of adhering to them in *Defigning*, and the Practice of *Architecture*, that they require no farther Explanation.

The Ground Work of the Whole arifes from the Beauty or Purity, and Simplicity, of Defigning : By *Purity*, I mean, free from being corrupted, Exactnefs, and Unmixednefs ; and by *Simplicity*, Plainnefs, and without Difguife. Thefe come next under my Confideration : Purity, as it relates to Architecture, is to be underftood as it was in its original State, when the Art was perfected ; and I think this may be traced, and proved to have exifted in Perfection in *Greece*, above two thoufand Years fince, and long before the Building of *Rome*.

Pliny, in Lib. xxxvi. Chap. 4. fays " That two hundred Years before the Deftruction of *Troy*, a School was founded at *Athens*, for the Inftruction and Encouragement of *Architects*, about A. M. 2600."

Diodorus, in his 4th Book, fays " That *Dedolus* fled from *Crete* to *Sicily*, to fave himfelf from the Anger of *Minos*, and was there received by *Gonfales*, King of that Ifland, whom he inftructed in the firft Principles of *Architecture*, about A. M. 2645."

Plutarch tells us, in his Life of *Pericles*, " That he was one of the greateft Lovers of *Architecture* among the *Grecians*, and was fo careful in the Edifices which he caufed to be built at *Athens*, that at the Time of *Trajan*, wherein *Plutarch* wrote, they feemed to be as newly done." And *Pliny*, Lib. xxxvi. Chap. 6. fays, " The Excellency of the *Grecian Architecture* was fo great, that *Scylla* caufed the *Columns* of the Temple of *Jupiter Olympus*, built at *Athens*, to be taken away to adorn the Temple of *Jupiter Capitelinus* at *Rome*.

I hope the Reader will pardon this hiftorical Digreffion. I have been more particular in it, to fhew, that it was in Perfection in *Greece* long before the Building of *Rome*, and four hundred and fixty Years before the Time of *Marcellus*; and then the *Romans* had not a true Relifh or Tafte of *Architecture*, till he conquered *Sicily*, from whence he brought the Art in Perfection to *Rome*.

From the Time of *Marcellus* to this Hour, I do not find a fingle Beauty has been, or could be, added to the three *Greek* Orders, nor a Decoration to

heighten

heighten or perfect either. The *Romans* indeed, added two other, which I wifh were namelefs, Orders : The *Tufcan*, funk into Dulnefs and Heavinefs in Compofition, and indeed not greatly unlike the *Doric* Order, except in the Want of *Neatnefs*, *Proportion*, and *Beauty :* The other is the *Roman*, or *Compofite Order*, confifting of a Redundancy of Mouldings, and the Capital fo maffy to the *Corinthian*, that it deferves no Comparifon with it.

I have now fhewn the Purity and Perfection of the *Grecian Architecture*, which *Vitruvius* and other great Geniufes practifed in *Rome*, and tranfmitted down to us, through all the Impediments of Novelty and Barbarity, through the Devaftations of *Gothic* Wildnefs, and which ftill fhines fuperior in Beauty and Excellence, to every other chimerical Innovation. It is this Purity I would recommend the Practice of to all concerned in the Study of Architecture. Let them diveft themfelves of Prejudice, and tell me if they ever have feen a Compofition of *Architecture* fo graceful and pleafing as the *Doric* and *Ionic* Orders; or fo beautifully perfect in Proportion and Ornament as the *Corinthian*.

Redundancy of Members, Ornament, and Drefs, are the Productions of unthinking Geniufes. Undecorated Plainnefs (as I obferved in my Preface) in a well proportioned Building, will ever pleafe. Study Nature and the *Grecian Architecture*, and you will be fure fo to improve, as feldom to fail of Succefs. If you trace the *pure* and *clear* Mirror up to *Vitruvius*, you will find every *Grace* and *Beauty* fhine forth in Perfection, and where any of the Orders are not introduced in Defigning, I recommend the laft Ingredient. *Simplicity*, *Plainnefs* and *Neatnefs*, with juft *Proportion*, is now all that is neceffary to be underftood by the Defigner, when that is in view, rather appropriating the Structure to *Ufe* and *Convenience*, than to *Shew* and *Ornament*. That I may not be mifunderftood in my Application of the Term *Simplicity*; that the Defigner is wholly to be reftricted to an univerfal Plainnefs, I muft beg Leave to obferve, that Decoration, is, in fome Meafure, a juft Effential to Beauty; but the great End of Appropriation terminates in Convenience: Your Structure muft anfwer the End for which it was erected, and the Ornament be fuited to the Dignity of the Inhabitant; but all fuch additional Embellifhments fhould be rather the Intent of internal than external Gaiety.

The Fancy of a young Defigner may flow into Luxuriancy; the Starts and Sallies of an unreftricted Genius may inadvertently lofe Sight of Nature; as when the Portal to a *Prifon* may be of the *Corinthian*, and that of a *Palace* be the *Tufcan Order*. Feftoons of Fruit and Flowers have been the Wildnefs of Fancy in a Seat near the Sea; and a Pavillion in a Flower-Garden has been group'd with Variety of *Fifh*, &c. In fhort, unnatural Productions are the Things I would mark out for avoiding in Defign, fo as to make the Reverfe more to be ftudied, and every Structure, to whatever

End

End raifed, to be confidered as to its *Ufe*, *Situation* and *Proportion*; and to make Art fit and tally with Nature in the Execution, fo that they may be equally fubfervient to each other.

But, before a Perfon begins to build, it is highly neceffary he fhould nearly know the Expence of the *Structure*; but often, through the Ignorance, or Defign, of the *Eftimator*, it exceeds *double*, fometimes *treble*, the Sum eftimated, and perhaps the Builder, when the Cortex or Shell only is covered in, finds himfelf incapable of finifhing. Sometimes the Burden more juftly falls on the *Eftimator*, who contracts to perform the Work for a Quarter lefs than the Value; but in both Cafes the *Eftimator* is equally blameable: If they are not capacitated to do it, let them employ People of Genius and Experience, and I dare affirm an infinite Number of BLUNDERS, *&c.* of this Kind would be prevented.

Vitruvius, in the firft Section, Book 10, fays, " That at *Ephefus*, one of the greateft and moft celebrated Cities of *Greece*, there was formerly a very fevere but juft Law, by which Architects, who undertook to furvey a public Work, was obliged to declare what it would coft, and to do the Work for the Price they demanded, and obliged themfelves by Bond of what they were worth. When the Work was done, they were rewarded with public Honour, if the Expence was as reported: If it did not amount by a Quarter Part of the Report, the Surplus was to be expended in public Works; but if it exceeded *more* than a Fourth of the Eftimate, that Excefs was to be furnifhed by the *Architect*."

" He fays alfo, it is to be wifhed, that at *Rome* fome fuch Rules for Buildings, efpecially *public*, were eftablifhed: This would impeach an infinite Number of ignorant, and unpunifhed Pretenders to *Architecture*; they would be prevented from running People to unknown, and unneceffary Expences, for Fear of the Penalty of the Law, and from diffembling or concealing the Expences neceffary to compleating the Work; and by this means thofe who would expend 400 Crowns (that was in the Time of *Vitruvius*) would have the Pleafure of feeing the Work perfected; but when they find in the Execution, that Sum is only half of what is fufficient, or what they refolved to lay out, they lofe Courage, and are often conftrained to abandon the Work they have undertaken." I have only to add, that I join with *Vitruvius* in wifhing fome fuch Law was in Force in *England*.

I have run this Introduction to a greater Length than I at firft intended I fhall therefore no longer detain you from the Work. As Tafte varies and is as different in each Man as *Features* and *Complexion*, I have, by my Specimens exhibited before the Publication, experienced *that* Change: Every one almoft differed in their Sentiments, even to the Appropriation and Ufe of the *Defign*. With Attention I heard them, fometimes altered

a Plate

a Plate, till *Reason* and Necessity forced me to reply, with *Pope* in his *Essay on Criticism*,

> " 'Tis hard to say, if greater Want of Skill
> " Appear in writing, or in judging ill:
> " But, of the two, less dang'rous is th' Offence
> " To tire our Patience, than mislead our Sense.
> " Some few in that, but Numbers err in this;
> " Ten censure wrong, for one who writes amiss.
> " 'Tis with our Judgment, as our Watches, none
> " Go just alike, yet each believes his own."

I submit the Performance to General and *Impartial Judges*, nor do I wish it longer to exist, than *those* are pleased to approve it.

R. MORRIS.

AN
EXPLANATION
OF THE
PLATES, &c.

PLATE I. A LITTLE plain Building 30 Feet in Front, 30 Feet in Depth, and 30 Feet high, to the Top of the Cornice, from Outside to Outside of the Walls on the Plan.—The Parlour and Chamber-floors 9 Feet 6 Inches high, and the Attick Story 8 Feet high; the other Proportions (*as in all the rest of the Plates,*) may be found by the Scale annexed thereto. This Building may be executed for the Sum of 324*l.*

PLATE II. The Square of the Building contains in Front 64 Feet, and 56 Feet in Depth, and the Front and Back Break for Part of the Octagon, 12 Feet each.—The Parlour-floor is 14 Feet, and the Chamber-floor 12 Feet high.— A Gallery goes all round the middle Room, on the Chamber-floor, to communicate privately with each Room and the Staircases.—A Colonade might be added in the Middle, leading from the Staircases to Offices on each Side the House, if required. This Building may be done in a good Manner for the Sum of 2860*l.*

PLATE III. A Building proposed to be erected on the South Downs in *Sussex.*—The 2 Fronts alike, one facing the *Sea*, the other enclosed with a Garden, and to the Downs; it was proposed for a single Gentleman.—The Extent of the House, Court, and Offices are 160 Feet. To execute this Building in a workmanlike Manner it will amount to the Sum of 680 *l.*

PLATE IV. A Seat for a Garden proposed for Retirement.
" Where purling Rills, and Aromatick Sweets,
" In unfrequented Gloom, diffusive spread,
" And met a mingled Wilderness of Flowers:
" The *Violet*, *Junquil*, and *Blushing-Rose*.
" Delicious Fragrance !———— Beauties to chear the Eye,
" Of various Texture, and a thousand Hue's,
" And Shades, and mazy Walks unknown to Fame.
The Expence of this Seat will amount to 24 *l.*

PLATE

PLATE V. A Seat 60 Feet in Front, 51 Feet deep, lower Offices 7 Feet 6 Inches high. Principal Floor 11 Feet, and Chamber-Story 9 Feet high.—Offices contiguous thereto muft be fuppofed proportioned, and convenient to the Dignity of the Inhabitant. To finifh this Building according to this Defign it will amount to the Sum of 2172 *l.*

PLATES VI. and VII. A Plan and Elevation of the Corinthian Order, extends 138 Feet, the lower Offices are propofed 9 Feet, the principal Floor 17 Feet, and the Attick Story 11 Feet high each, in the Clear. The Coft of this Building, according to this Defign, will amount to the Sum of 5331 *l.* 5 *s.*

PLATE VIII. *An Adytum*, 12 Feet Diameter. This Plate, to the facetious Mr. *Daniel Garrett*, ARCHITECT, is dedicated. The Ufe of thefe Retreats in ancient Times, are now generally known, my Friend above-mentioned, upon feeing fome Specimens of this Work, was pleafed jocofely to intimate, that my Title RURAL ARCHITECTURE, was not juftly appropriated, becaufe I had not any where introduced any Trees.—His kind Hint led me to form this little *Sanctum Sanctorum* for him.—I have enclofed it on 3 Sides, with *Shrubs* and *Ever-Greens*, to fuit it for a Retirement in a calm Summer Evening, where divefted of Care, and the agonizing Pains of the Gout, and of all other real and *imaginary Maladies*, with a few felected Friends, may he enjoy all the Happinefs and Tranquility, that they or himfelf can wifh to poffefs.
Homo fum, humani nihil a me alienum puto.
This Seat may be built for the Sum of 75 *l.*

PLATES IX. and X. A Plan and Profile of a little Garden-Houfe, fuppofed to command fome beautiful Profpect from the Top.—The principal Room is 30 Feet long, by 20 Feet wide, and 18 Feet high. The back Rooms, only 11 Feet high, with an Attick over them 7 Feet 6 Inches high ; and the Staircafe leading to the Turret.—The Drefs is plain and fimple, and only the proper Decoration of the Order, and Situation of the Structure. To compleat this Building according to this Defign, will amount to 607 *l.* 10 *s.*

PLATE XI. A plain Structure, the Body of the Houfe is 70 Feet fquare, the Parlour-floor 14 Feet high, Chamber 12 Feet, and Attick Story 9 Feet high ; the Colonade of the Ionick Order extends on each Side 50 Feet, and the *Kitchen*, and *Stable-Buildings*, beyond, are in Front each 30 Feet,——making in the whole Range 230 Feet. The Coft of this Building with its Offices and Colonades amounts to the Sum of 2953 *l.* 16 *s.*

PLATE XII. A Pavillion intended to terminate the Boundaries of a Garden, on an Eminence, where an agreeable Profpect may be had round the Horizon.——The internal Part is an Octagon 24 Feet Diameter, and 15 Feet high, and the 2 Side Parts 10 Feet fquare, and coved.——I made fo many Windows in it, for the more eafy obtaining a Variety of Views. This may be built for the Sum of 352 *l.* 16 *s.*

PLATE XIII. A Plan and Profile of a little Houfe, 40 Feet fquare from Out to Out ; lower Offices are to be fuppofed, and 7 Feet and half high, and the Height of the Parlour and Chamber-floor, each 13 Feet. Convenient Out-houfes may be added, proportioned to the Ufes of a fmall Family, for which this was defigned. The Coft of this Building will amount to the Sum of 880 *l.*

PLATES XIV. and XV. A Garden-Seat, or additional Room to a Building, where a Communication might be had to it, on the Chimney Side next the Venetian Window, or to be placed at the End of an Avenue in a Garden, either for Profpect to diftant Objects, or as an Object to be viewed from a Diftance.——The Room is propofed to be 24 Feet fquare, and 20 Feet high ; the Columns of the Portico are 2 Feet Diameter, and

10 Diameters high. To finish this Building, according to the Design, it will amount to 660 *l*.

PLATE XVI. Confifts of a Plan and Profile of a Building, the central Part of which is 55 Feet in Front, on each Side of it, an Arcade 30 Feet in Length, and at each End of thofe, are Offices 32 Feet each in Front, the whole Length extending 179 Feet.—— The Parlour-Story is 12 Feet, the Chamber 9 Feet, and the Attick-Story 8 Feet high in the Clear. The whole Coft of this Houfe and Offices will amount to the Sum of 1369 *l*.

PLATE XVII. A Room intended for a Cold Bath, the middle Part is 27 Feet long, 20 Feet broad, and 20 Feet high in the Clear. The 2 Sides are 12 Feet by 9 and 12 Feet high, and groyned on the top Part. This Building will amount to the Sum of 367 *l*.

PLATE XVIII. This Plan of the principal Floor, and Profile of the Corinthian Order, is defigned for a Villa, having each Front open—The principal Front and oppofite are alike, and extend each 100 Feet, the Depth is 110 Feet, and the oppofite Front the fame. I propofe the principal Approaches to the 2 principal Fronts, by large Avenues afcending thereto, and the proper Offices laying enclofed on each Side the two oppofite Avenues enclofed by a circular Colonade, infcribing the Breadth of the two principal Fronts. The lower Offices are 9 Feet high, the principal Floor 18 Feet, and the Attick Story 11 Feet high, each in the Clear. The whole Expence of this Building according to this Defign amounts to 9400 *l*.

PLATE XIX. A little Seat, or refting Place at the End of a Walk or Avenue, or to terminate a View, or hide fome difagreeable Object.—It is merely the Child of Fancy, and may be deftined to what Ufe the judicious Reader fhall think moft proper. This Seat may be Built for 30 *l*.

PLATE XX. A Plan and Profile of a plain Seat, with the Offices, which extend 256 Feet.—The middle Part, or Body of the Houfe, is 70 Feet, the Paffages and Offices on each Side between the Stables, &c. are 73 Feet each, and the Stable, and Brew-houfe Buildings, each 20 Feet,—The Depth of the middle Part of the Houfe is 52 Feet,— the Parlour-floor 12 Feet, Chamber 10 Feet, and Attick Story 8 Feet high. I propofe the Kitchen to go through 2 Stories, and will be twenty Feet high. To execute this Building in a well finifh'd Manner it will amount to the Sum of 3757 *l*. 10 *s*.

PLATE XXI. A twin Brother to Plate 19, and teemed at one Birth; its Utility, (however illuminated) may be the fame or fubfervient in many Ufes; I have confidered only the Proportion, Uniformity of Parts, and Difpofition of the whole, leaving abler Judges to nominate its Ufe. This may be built for 34 *l*.

PLATES XXII. and XXIII. A Plan and Profile of the Ionick Order, of a Villa, 220 Feet in Front, and 105 Feet in Depth, the Profiles are the *Portico* fuppofed to the South, the other to the North Afpect.—The lower Offices are 10 Feet, the principal Floor 16 Feet, and the Attick Story 9 Feet high in the Clear, the Hall is 40 Feet by 30, and 24 Feet high.—And the Saloon to the other Front, 50 Feet by 40, and the fame Height to the Cove, and coved above that a Quarter of that Height.—The *Tribune*, or *Paffage*, or *Veftible*, between thefe Rooms, is the general Communication to the Staircafes on each Floor, which with the Paffages are illuminated from each Court, on the Sides of the Stairs, the Convenience of which are more intelligibly defcribed by the Plan and Scale thereto annexed. To finifh this Building in a good Manner according to this Defign, it will amount to the Sum of 16400 *l*.

PLATE

PLATE XXIV. This little Building I intended for a private cold Bath: An Octagon of 12 Feet Diameter, and 12 Feet high, the Bottoms of the Niches to be about 3 Feet from the Floor, and about 2 Feet below the general Surface of the Water, proposed to be about 4 Feet or 4 Feet and a half high, the Recesses or external Niches to have a circular Seat at each End,——Contiguous to this may be added, a Dressing Room, either separated from, or joined to the Building, or may have a Communication to any Apartment of a House, at the place where the Niche is, facing the Door; if more Light is required, that may be easily obtained. The Expence of this little Building will amount to 80 *l*.

PLATE XXV. A Seat 200 Feet in Front,——the principal Floor 20 Feet high and coved,—to the other Front, (which is separated from the Principal, or Garden front by a middle Wall,) is 12 Feet high on the Principal Floor, and an Attick Story over it 8 Feet. So that no Rooms are proposed over the State Rooms.——The lower Offices under the whole, to be 8 Feet high in the Clear,—and illuminated from both Fronts, that proposed the Principal or Garden-front to have no Windows, in the general View, but the Top of them, a little below the Surface of the Ground, and enclosed by a Curb sunk as low as the Bottom of the Windows.——To the Apartments in the other Front, the Windows may appear 2 Feet above the Surface of the Ground, supposing the Ground of that Front to lie 2 Feet lower than the Principal.——Offices suitable to the House, in Magnitude and Convenience, are to be properly adapted, and may be easily added thereto, joined either by a square or circular Colonade, or Arcades, on each Side to the Front opposite to the principal, making the common Entrance to the House at the Rooms at the Ends of the lower Offices. This Building may be finish'd for the Sum of 5625 *l*.

PLATE XXVI. The Offspring of Plate IV. the Use and Composition is homogeneal; and shew them analogous in the Form, but with a Variety in the little Parts of which it is composed. This little Seat may be built for 20 *l*.

PLATES XXVII. and XXVIII. A Plan of the Principal Floor, and plain Profile of the Corinthian Order of a Seat 125 Feet in Front, and 50 Feet in Depth; the lower Offices are 8 Feet, the principal Story 16 Feet, and the Attick Story, 12 Feet high in the Clear. All the outer and subordinate Offices are supposed only such as the Wants and natural Conveniences of the Inhabitants of such a Structure require; and so disposed of, as to have an easy Communication. according to the several Subserviences, and Uses to which they shall be appropriated.—I shall here make one general Observation for this, and all the other *Designs*, where the Offices are supposed only, and not *delineated*, that the Smallness of the Plates render it impossible to add, so as to make them intelligible, without double or folding Plates, and also, besides that Inconvenience, as the Offices are only as the subordinate Part of the Structure, the Principal being settled, little Difficulty will attend the designing of them: Because, it is to be always understood, that there is Ground or Space enough for the Designer to exercise his Fancy. The Cost of this Building will amount to 4655 *l*.

PLATE XXIX. This Plan and Profile is proposed for a Keeper's Lodge, or Garden House, and to be placed in some advantageous Situation, for commanding a View of the Park or Garden, from the Arcade. The inner Wall of the Arcade goes no higher than the Ground-floor, so that the Chambers will be so much longer as the Thickness of that Wall, and the Breadth of the Arcade, when the Passage and Arcade are included above; one of the Rooms will be 22 Feet square, the other 22 Feet by 15,—and the Chimneys, if required, be placed in the Centre of each Room, the Ground-floor is 10 Feet, and the Chamber 9 Feet high. The Expence of this Building will amount to 560 *l*.

Feet

PLATE XXX. The general Conſtruction of this Plan is formed from a Square of 45 Feet *from out to out,* and the inſcribing Part of 4 Octagons, 22 Feet Diameter in the Clear; 3 Sides of each of theſe Octagons break beyond the ſquare Part 7 Feet, the other Sides forming 5 Spaces, each 8 Feet 6 Inches ſquare, as is more particularly deſcribed by the Plan.—The Profile is plain and ſimple,—The Ground or Parlour is 13 Feet, and the Chambers 10 Feet high in the Clear, the middle Square or Veſtible is illuminated in each Story from the Staircaſe.—The Situation for this Structure ſhould be on an Eminence whoſe Summit ſhould overlook a long extended Vale, and, if attainable, quite round the Horizon, ſo that each Room is an eaſy and quick Tranſition to ſome new Object, ſuch a Spot would be habitable only a Part of the Year, Summer's extream Heat, and Winter's bleak and piercing Cold and Winds, would render it an uncomfortable or diſagreeable Reſidence; nor is it indeed any way ſuited but for a very ſmall Family, and few Attendants, though Offices under the Ground, and a Foſs round the Houſe might be very eaſily attained. This Houſe may be built for 1000 *l.*

PLATES XXXI. and XXXII. The Plan and Profile of the Ionick Order, of an octangular *Temple* or *Chapel,* 60 Feet the outer Diameter, and the internal 40 Feet, and the outer Iſle 6 Feet wide, the internal Wall which ſupports the Dome, I ſuppoſe the ſame Thickneſs as the external, and the Arches or Openings in it 10 Feet Diameter, and 20 Feet high; from the 6 Windows, and thoſe over them, and the Chancel End, there will be ſufficient Light: I do not propoſe any Gallery,—from the Pavement within, to the Inſide of the Roof 45 Feet high.—It has been objected to, that the inner Part ſhould have been a Circle in the Plan, and the Roof ſpherical, that the Sound ſtriking in the Angles, will render it confuſed, and reverberate from a Roof Octangular in the Plan, very unintelligible to the Audience; but as the Angles are ſmall, and nearly approaching to a Circle, I think the Objection of little Weight, however, I refer this nice Point to the judicious in *Muſick* and *Sounds* to explain, contenting myſelf with *Pope's* Reflection, in his Eſſay on Criticiſm.

" Whoever thinks a faultleſs Piece to ſee,
" Thinks what ne'er was, nor is, nor e'er ſhall be."

To execute this Building, according to this Deſign, it will amount to 2561 *l.* 16 *s.*

PLATE XXXIII. A little Farm-Houſe, and convenient Out-houſes for a ſmall Dairy; the Parlour or Ground Floor in the ſquare Part or Body of the Houſe is 11 Feet high, and the Chamber-floor 9 Feet, the Rooms in the ſcaline Building 9 Feet and half high, the Reſt of the Building will be better explained by the Plan and Scale annexed. This Building with its Offices according to this Deſign will amount to 1100 *l.*

PLATES XXXIV. and XXXV. Half the Plan, and a Profile of one Side of a Town-Houſe, and Market-Houſe in the Form of a Croſs, of the Ionick Order, each Side regular and alike. The Extent from South to North, or from Eaſt to Weſt, is 128 Feet with a Piazza round the ſame 9 Feet wide in the Clear, over which is an open Walk encloſed with a Balluſtrade all round the Building on the Outſide.—The Room above is 98 Feet long, 32 Feet broad, and 20 Feet high, and including the Staircaſe is the ſame the other way;—this Room may be divided by temporary Partitions for the Buſineſs of the Borough, Corporation, &c. And occaſionally be enlarged for publick Utility, the Diſtribution of Juſtice, Concerts, Aſſemblies, &c.—The Walk within the Arcade below is 17 Feet in Height; the Columns are of the Ionick Order, 20 Inches Diameter, and 9 Diameters high, including the Baſe and Capitals. To build this, according to this Deſign, will amount to 7530 *l.*

PLATE XXXVI. A Plan and Profile of a plain Villa, 66 Feet in Front, and 56 Feet deep, the lower Offices are 8 Feet high, Parlour-floor 11 Feet, and the Attick or Chamber over it 9 Feet high, the Communications to the lower Offices are by Steps down on the Outſide to the 2 Staircaſes. This Building will amount to the Sum of 2220 *l.*

PLATE

PLATE XXXVII. A little Building intended for Retirement, or for a Study, to be placed in some agreeable Part of a Park or Garden, the middle Part is 34 Feet in Front and 40 Feet in Depth, and the 2 Scaline Buildings 16 Feet 6 Inches each in Front, and 34 Feet deep.—The Principal or Ground Floor is 16 Feet 6 Inches high, and the Attick 10 Feet, the opposite Front to that in the Plate is proposed to be without Drefs or Ornament, and a Door under the Stairs the common Communication. The whole Expence of this Building will amount to 1089*l*.

PLATE XXXVIII. A Green-Houfe;—This Building has no Communication with the back Part marked A B C, for that is only a Scalene or Lean-to, and the Top of the Roof to it comes under the Eves of the Green Houfe; which is 63 Feet long, 18 Feet broad, and 18 Feet high, South Afpect.—The Back or North Wall, has an *Undulating* or *winding Funnel* in it, 1 Foot high, and arched, and 9 Inches broad, and makes 3 Revolutions and Half in the Height of 18 Feet, and in the Center of the Building, the Shaft rifes above or behind the Roof.—The Room A is a *Stoke-Hole*, and a Place for *Peet* or *Tan*, which opens into and ferves the Funnel, there is 18 Inches Thicknefs of Brickwork next the Scalene Building, and but 4 Inches in the Funnels next the Green-Houfe, that it may receive the greater Heat, but that all the Parts of the Wall may receive an equal Warmth, I propofe perpendicular Cavities 4 Inches fquare, and about 2 Feet and half Diftance from each other, to go through, and crofs the great Funnel, from the Floor to the Cieling, unlefs in the lower Bottom, for there the Soot, would lodge and foon fill. And in order to clean the great Funnel, at the Ends of each Revolution of the fame, I would work the Funnel through, and ftop it with an upright Joint 3 Bricks thick to take out when wanted, and by a Rake or fuch Inftrument, might be cleaned from each End, and to keep the Smoke in the Funnels the longer, I would have a *Tin* or *Iron* Valve on a Curb at the Top of the Funnel, which the Smoke would eafily raife when too full: The Rooms B C a Bed-Chamber, and a Tool-Houfe forthe Gardener.—*N. B.* This Method I propofe for preferving very tender Plants *native* or *exotick*, which are often deftroyed through the Severity of fome Winter Seafons.—The Funnels of the Chimnies of the 2 Rooms, muft have no Communications with the *undulating* or *winding Funnels*, but muft have a Shaft feparate from it,—as I have no where feen thefe Things practifed, I only propofe it as a Scheme; and refer it to the Opinion of *Gardeners*, or better Judges to put in Execution. This Building may be finifh'd according to this Defign for 498 *l*.

PLATE XXXIX A Building propofed to be erected on an Eminence, for which Reafon, I made the Parlour-floor only 10 Feet high, and the Chamber 9 Feet; the Building is 60 Feet in Front, and 40 Feet deep, and has nothing but its Plainnefs to recommend it, for if the *Pilafters* and *Pediment* were omitted, as in the other Front is propofed, the Compofition is fimple in the Extream.—The Offices lay on each Side the Houfe.——The Communication to which is under the Staircafes, by a *Colonade* of the Ionick Order, of 35 Feet in Length, and the Difpofition of thofe Offices muft be fuppofed adequate, and in Proportion and Utility to the Convenience of the Inhabitants. The Coft of this Building will amount to 2100*l*.

PLATE XL. A Plan and Profile of a Bridge of Stone, the Water Way extending 132 Feet, the Stream is fuppofed navigable for fmall Veffels, the middle Arch is 35 Feet broad, and 25 Feet in Height from the Surface of the Water, at the common or general Height marked A, excepting fuppofed *Drought* or *Floods*.
B—The Surface of the Ground, about 5 Feet below the Surface of the Water.
C—The Bottom or Bed of the Pier, about 5 Feet blow the Surface of the Ground.
D D, &c.—The Plan of Half the Length of the Bridge, reprefenting the Piers at the Surface of the Ground.
E—Half of the upper Part or Way on the Bridge for Carriages, &c.
F F—A Way on each Side 4 Feet Broad, with Pofts fet for the Safety of the Foot-Paffengers.

g g The

g g—The Parapet Walls, or Breaſt Work, which encloſe the Sides of the Bridge.

As to the Method of erecting, or Building *Bridges*, you may conſult the re-
nowned, *Monſieur Palapance, Bridge-Builder* to the two Kings of *Brentford*, in that
wonderful *Puerile Treatiſe* of HIS entitled, *Remarks on the different Conſtructions of
Bridges*, &c. publiſhed 1749————*Meliora pii docuere Parentes.* Hor.

PLATE XLI. A Bridge propoſed for a River, whoſe Water Way extends 226 Feet,
the Piers to be of Stone, and the Superſtructure on the Piers propoſed to be of Timber,
one half of the Plan ſhews the Piers above the Surface of the Ground, as the Plan in Plate
XL;—and the other half, the Way on the Piers which in the middle Part is 36 Feet
wide, and on the other Sides of it 30 Feet wide, the middle Part breaks 3 Feet on each
Side for the Safety of Paſſengers, and the eaſier Paſſage of the Carriages paſſing and
repaſſing, &c.—The Reſt of the Explanation, I refer you to the laſt Plate for the Piers,
&c. Or the Scale hereto annexed.

PLATES XLII. and XLIII. A Plan and Profile of a Building for a Garden or Sum-
mer-Houſe, the Length each Way, between the Pilaſters within ſide, is 40 Feet, and
the Breadth between the Pilaſters 17 Feet, and the Height to the Spring of the Dome
16 Feet, and the Dome within Side is a Semiſphere of 18 Feet Diameter, which may
be raiſed from the under Side of the Cornice in the Room without Columns, they being
placed there more for Ornament than Uſe.—It was deſigned for an ornamental Termi-
nation of a Walk, or for Proſpect, or an Evening's Repaſt in a Garden, &c. The
Expence of this Building will amount to the Sum of 997 *l*. 10 *s*.

PLATE XLIV. A Plan and plain Profile of a Market or Town-Houſe extending
76 Feet in Length, and 38 Feet in Breadth, in the middle Part, and from the Paving
to the Top of the blocking Courſe 34 Feet high, the Room over it from the Stairs, to
the dotted Line marked A, is 48 Feet in Length, 30 Feet wide, and 18 Feet high,
and the remaining Length of the Room is 11 Feet.—A Chimney is propoſed to be in
the Center above, and a blank Receſs on the Outſide to preſerve the Uniformity.—
The Room may ſerve for various Purpoſes in a Borough or Corporation-Town, for
Muſick, Aſſemblies, &c. as well as the general Adminiſtration of Juſtice, &c. This
Building may be compleated according to this Deſign for 1200 *l*.

PLATE XLV. A plain Church for a Village, 50 Feet long in the Clear, and 45 Feet
wide in the broadeſt Part, and from the Pavement to the Cieling 23 Feet high.—The
Extent in Length, from the Outſide of the Tower to the End of the Chancel, is 80
Feet.—The Height of the ſquare Part of the Tower from the Ground is 40 Feet, the
Octagon Part above is 15 Feet Diameter, and 18 Feet high to the Top of the Battlements, and the Spire 45 Feet above the Battlements. The Spire is propoſed to be of
Timber, and covered with Lead, the Pews will contain about 150 Perſons, for a Village a great Diſtance from Town, where modern Hoops are not uſed, otherwiſe it
would not eaſily hold 50. The whole Expence of Building this Church will amount
to the Sum of 1537 *l*.

PLATE XLVI A plain Altar-Piece of the Ionick Order, and ſuitable to the preceed-
ing Deſign, the Pedeſtal to the Order ſerves alſo, (by containing the Dado and Mouldings round,) as a Table Ornaments of Feſtoons; and Carving might be added, but the
pure Order without Decoration is more agreeable, and better appropriated to the
Structure, where a natural Simplicity has been endeavoured to be preſerved from an
Innundation of Dreſs and Gaiety. This Altar-Piece may be built for 30 *l*.

PLATE XLVII. The Oddity of this Deſign has a little puzzled me to determine its
Name and Uſes.—I have conſulted a very grave Jewiſh Rabbin, who informs me
very little is wanting to make it a compleat Synagogue.—An honeſt plain-meaning
Derviſs

Dervife commends it, and wifhes me to fend a Copy of it, (by him,) to *Conftantinople,* as a Model for a Mofque.

One zealous for the Propagation of his own Tenets, informs me, it is extremely well fuited for a Chapel, and its Confeffionals.——A Puritan of modern Growth entreats me not to make any Alteration in it, for it is the beft he could ever wifh to fee executed to perform their Devotions in.

I had the Curiofity to afk a young Surgeon, an ingenious Pupil of Mr. *B—m—fd*'s, and he affured me it would make an excellent private Diffecting-Room, and the adjoining Cells, as he calls them, a proper Repofitory for their Inftruments, and other Apparatus, &c. Mr. *L——gf—d* infifts it is the compleateft he ever faw for an Auction-Room. My Friend Mr. *S————* is of Opinion, that a fmall Alteration in 7 of the Entrances, by making the internal Opening 12 Feet wide, and converting the external Door of each into a Window, as at A A, would with proper Decorations, be a beautiful and compleat Building for a Library.

I can only fay my firft Intentions were to make it for a cold Bath, but as there are fo many Conjectures and Opinions about its Utility, I fhall fubmit it to better Judges, to affign a Ufe for it, moft agreeable to their own Sentiments. The whole Coft of this Building will not exceed 1260 *l.*

PLATES XLVIII. and XLIX. A plain Plan and Profile for a Church for a pretty populous Town, propofing to have a Gallery to the South and North Sides, as far as the Columns, and to return at the Weft End to the firft Column; the Length between the Walls of the Body of the Church is 71 Feet, and the Breadth between the Walls 77 Feet,—and the Chancel is 20 Feet fquare; from the Floor or Paving of the Church, to the under Side the Cieling under the Gallery, is 14 Feet, and from thence, the Pedeftal Column, and Entablature of the Ionick Order, to the Cieling of the Church, is 20 Feet, making the whole Height 34 Feet in the Clear. This Church may be built for 4370 *l.*

PLATE L. This octangular Plan and Profile of a fmall Pleafure-Room, I propofed to be placed on a Terrafs near *Windfor,* which has a very pleafing, and extenfive Profpect, almoft uninterrupted; 3 Fourths round the Horizon, and from which you may fee and trace at different Places, the Windings of the *Thames,* from *Maidenhead*-Bridge to *Richmond,* the Terrafs is on fuch an Eminence. A Building of this Kind would be an Object feen at a Diftance, and render it as well an Amufement to entertain the Fancy of others, as to thofe on the Spot, for a Variety of beautiful Hills, Vales, Landfkips, &c. for the Pleafure of the Inhabitants, create a new Succeffion of pleafing Images, and call forth the Beauty, Order, and Harmony of Nature, to decorate and enliven the Scene. This Building may be executed for 150 *l.*

Pl. 1.

Robertus Morris Architect! del. & inv.

Parr Sculp.

Pl. 2.

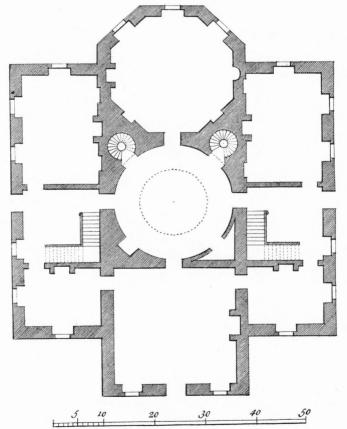

5   10   20   30   40   50

Robertus Morris Architect. del. & inv.   *Parr Sculp.*

Pl. 3.

Robertus Morris Architects inv. & del.

Parr Sculp.

Pl. 4.

1 2 3 4 5 6 7 8 9 10

Robertus Morris Architect. inv. & del.

Parr Sculp.

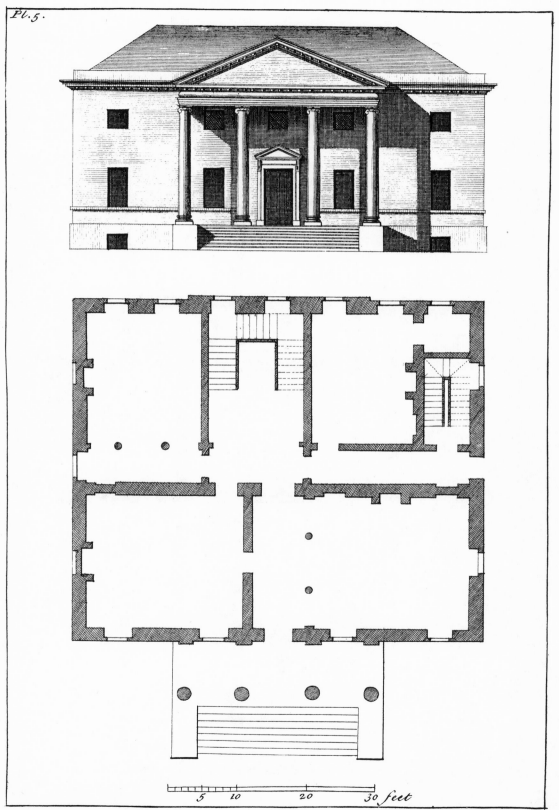

Pl. 5.

5   10   20   30 feet

Robertus Morris Architect.ⁱ inv. & del.   Parr Sculp

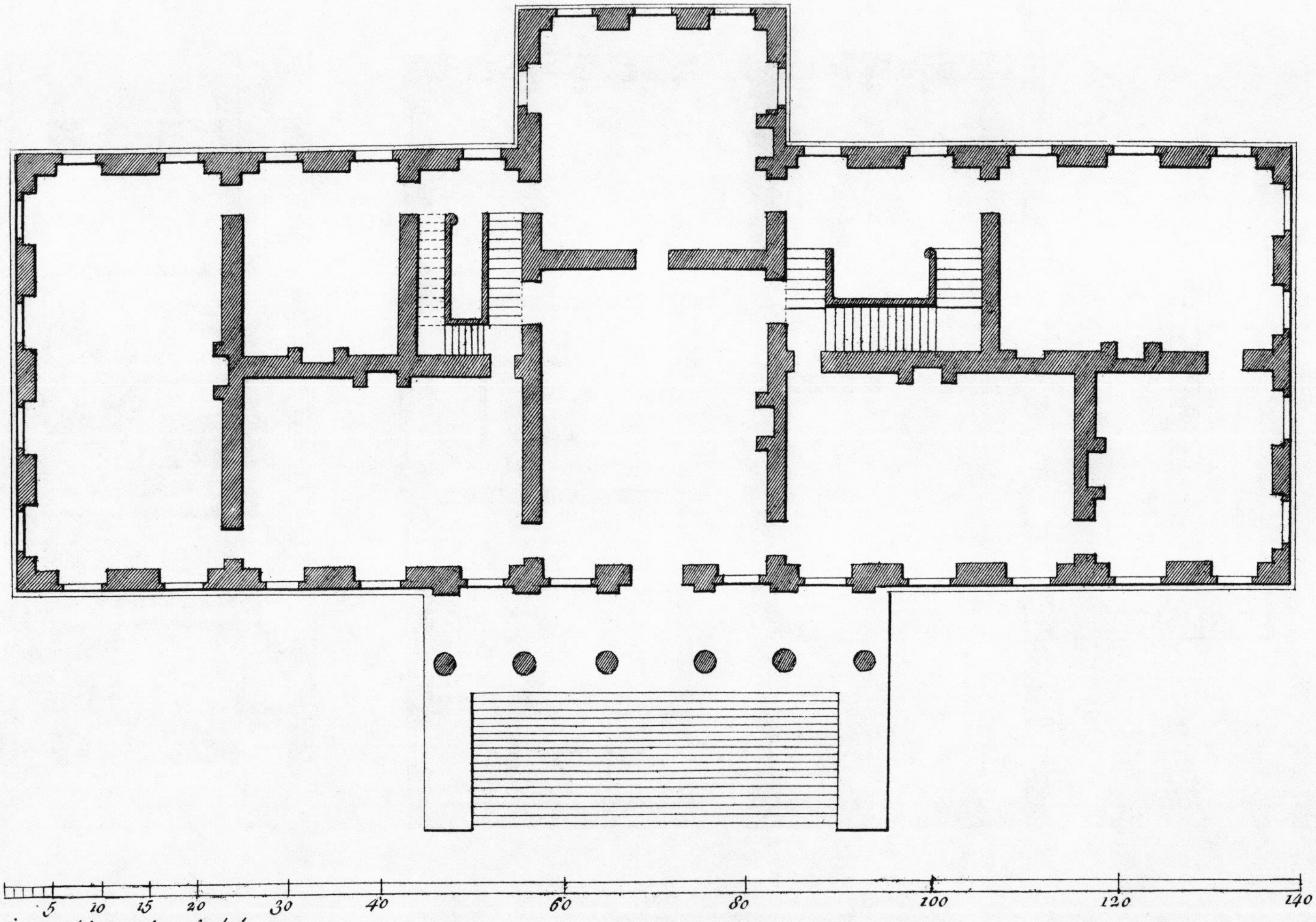

Pl. 6. to face Pl. 7.

Robertus Morris Architect: inv. & del.

Pl. 7.

Rob.t Morris inv. & del.

Parr Sculp

5 10 15 20 40 60 80 100 120 140

Pl. 8.

1 2 3 4 5   10   15   20

Robt. Morris inv. & del.   *Parr Sculp*

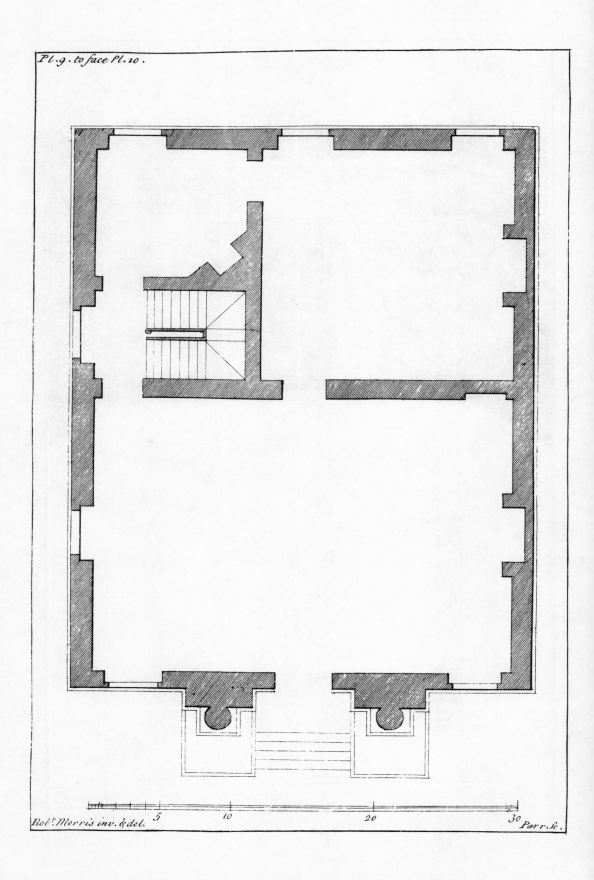

Pl. 9 . to face Pl. 10 .

Robt Morris inv. & del.

5   10   20   30 Parr Sc.

Pl. 10.

5   10   20   30 feet

Rob.t Morris inv & del.   Parr Sculp

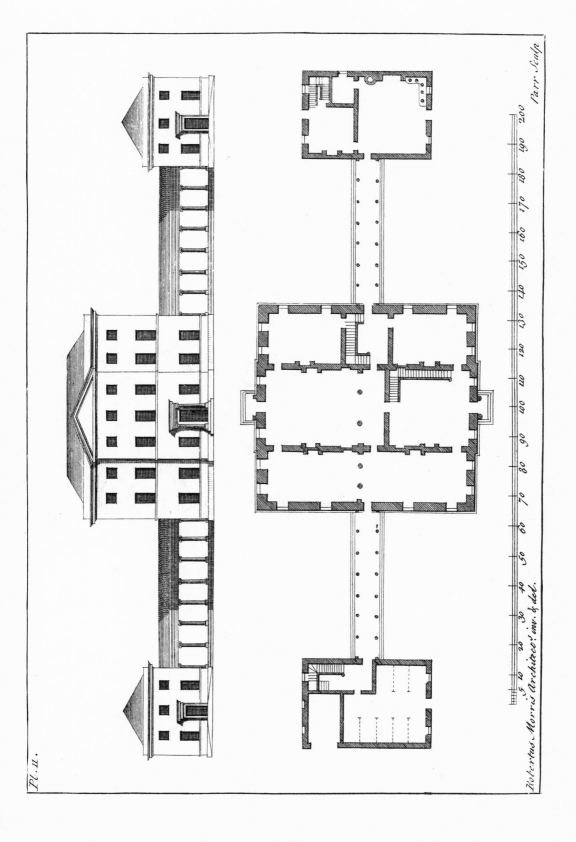

Pl. 11.

Robertus Morris Architect: inv: & del.

Parr: Sculp.

5 10 20 30 40 50 60 70 80 90 100 110 120 130 140 150 160 170 180 190 200

Pl. 12.

1. 2 3 4 5   10   15   20   30   40

Robt. Morris inv. & del.   Parr Sculp

Pl. 13.

5   10   20   30 f.

Rob.t Morris inv. & del.

Parr Sculp.

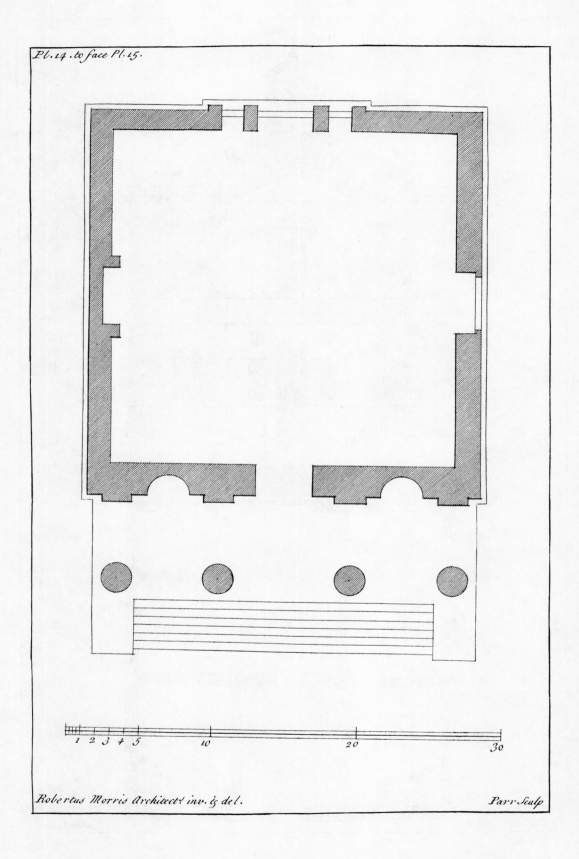

Pl. 14. to face Pl. 15.

1 2 3 4 5   10   20   30

Robertus Morris Architect: inv. & del.   Parr Sculp

Pl.15.

Robertus Morris Architect.? inv. & del.   *Parr Sculp*

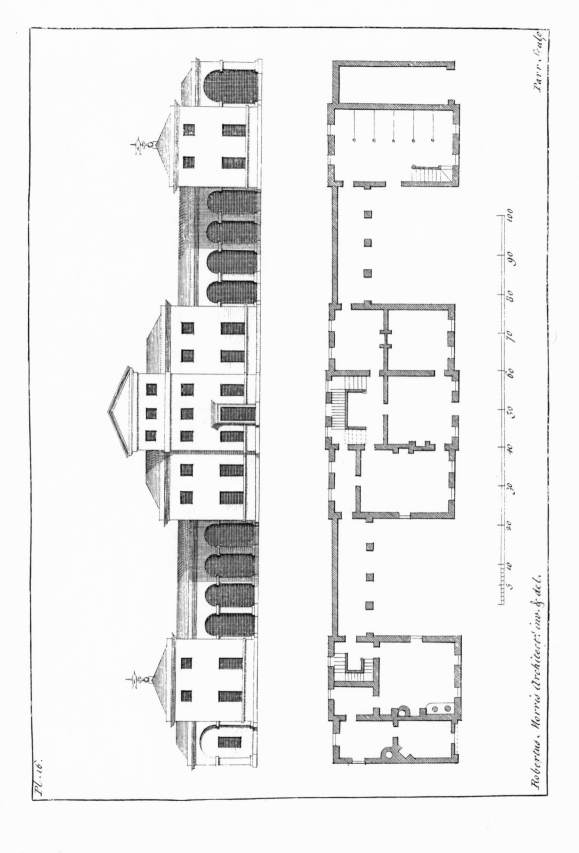

Pl. 16.

Robertus Morris Architect invt & del.

Parr Sculp

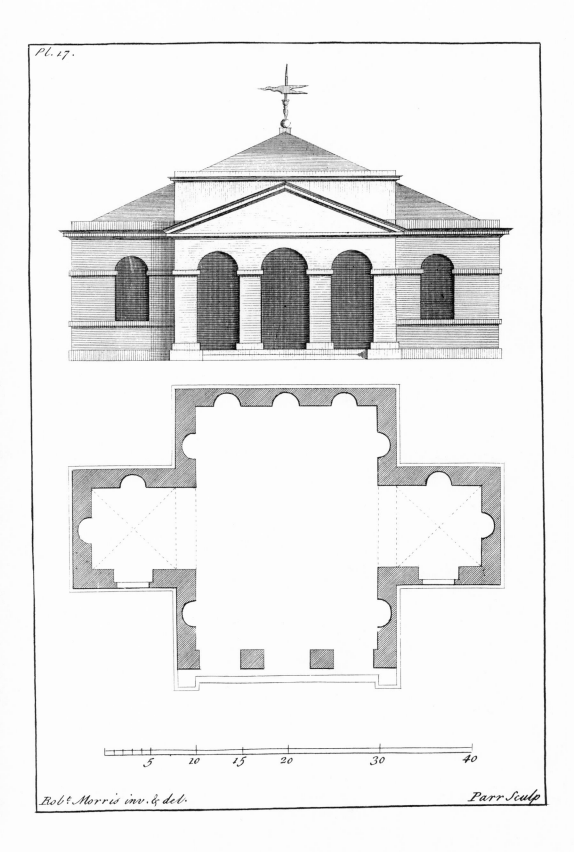

Pl. 17.

5   10   15   20   30   40

Robt. Morris inv. & del.   Parr Sculp

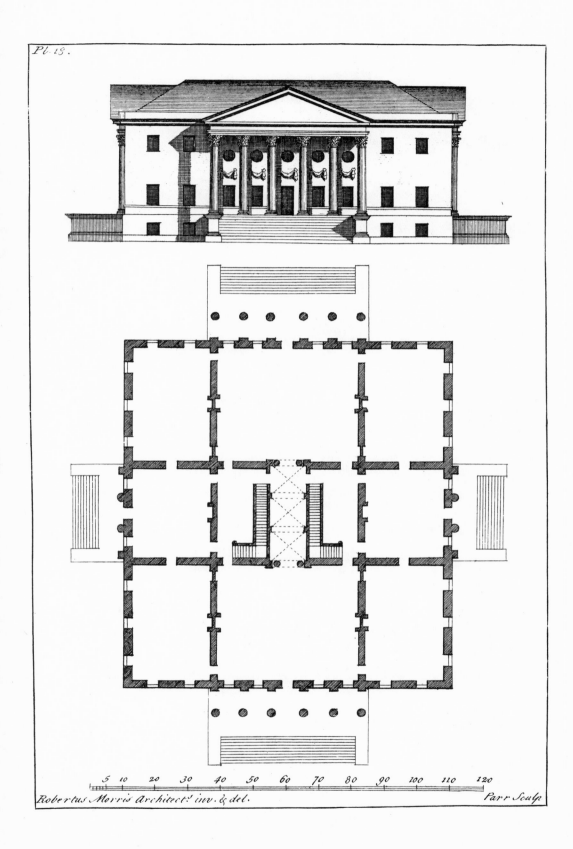

Pl. 13.

5 10 20 30 40 50 60 70 80 90 100 110 120

Robertus Morris Architect: inv. & del.   Parr Sculp

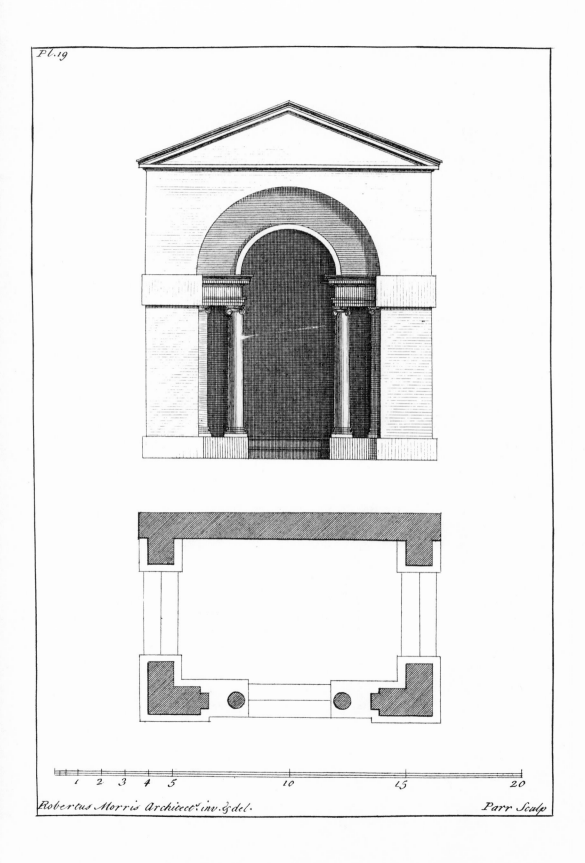

Pl. 19

1 2 3 4 5   10   15   20

Robertus Morris Architect.ʳ inv. & del.   *Parr Sculp*

Pl. 20.

Rob.t Morris inv.t & del.

Parr Sculp

5 10   20   40   60   80   100   120   140   160   180   200   220   240

Pl. 21.

Robertus Morris Architect! inv. & del.   *Parr Sculp*

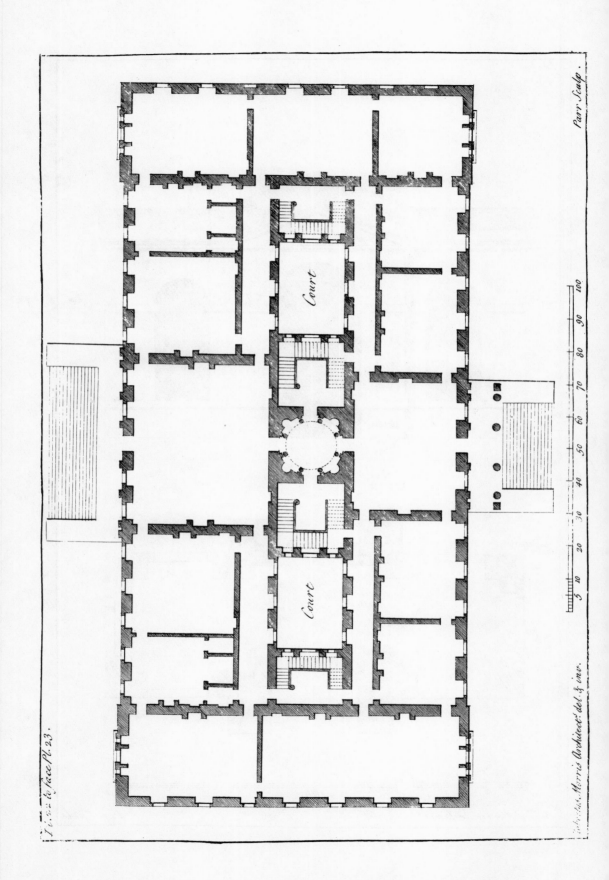

Court

Court

Parr Sculp.

Jonathan Harris Architect del. & inv.

5 10   20   30   40   50   60   70   80   90   100

Pl. 23

Parr. Sculp.

Robertus Morris Architectus delt. & inv.

Pl. 24.

Rob.t Morris inv. & del.

Parr Sculp

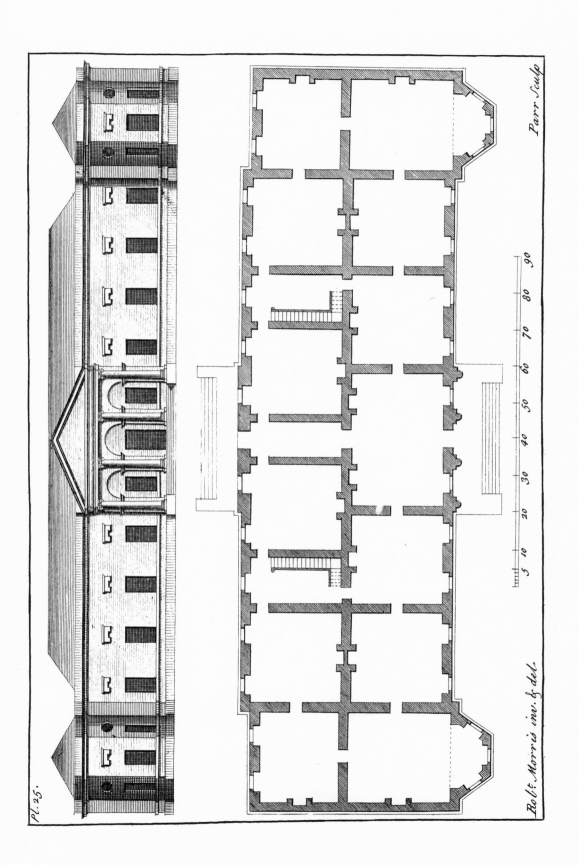

Pl. 25.

Parr Sculp

Rob.t Morris inv. & del.

5 10   20   30   40   50   60   70   80   90

Pl. 26.

Pl. 27. to face Pl. 28.

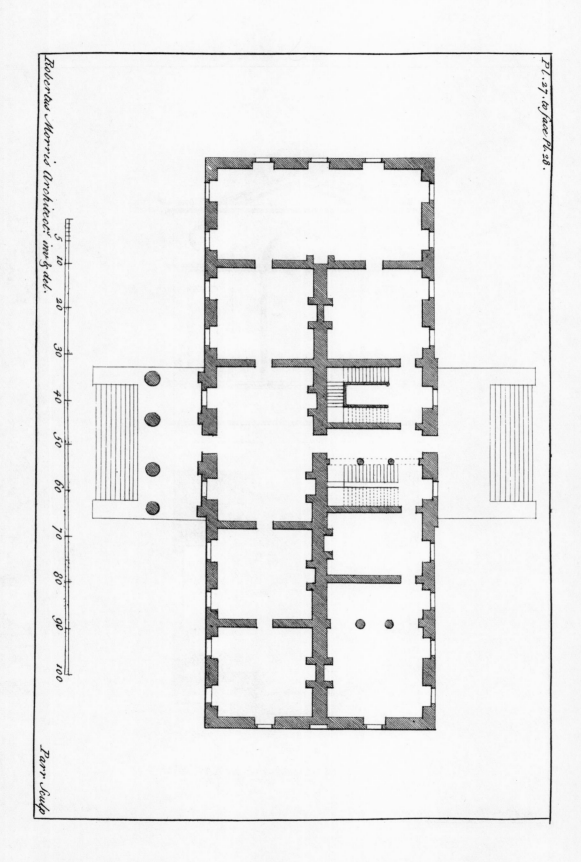

Robertus Morris Architect inv. & del.

Parr Sculp

5 10 20 30 40 50 60 70 80 90 100

Pl. 26.

Robertus Morris Architect: inv: & del.

Parr Sculp

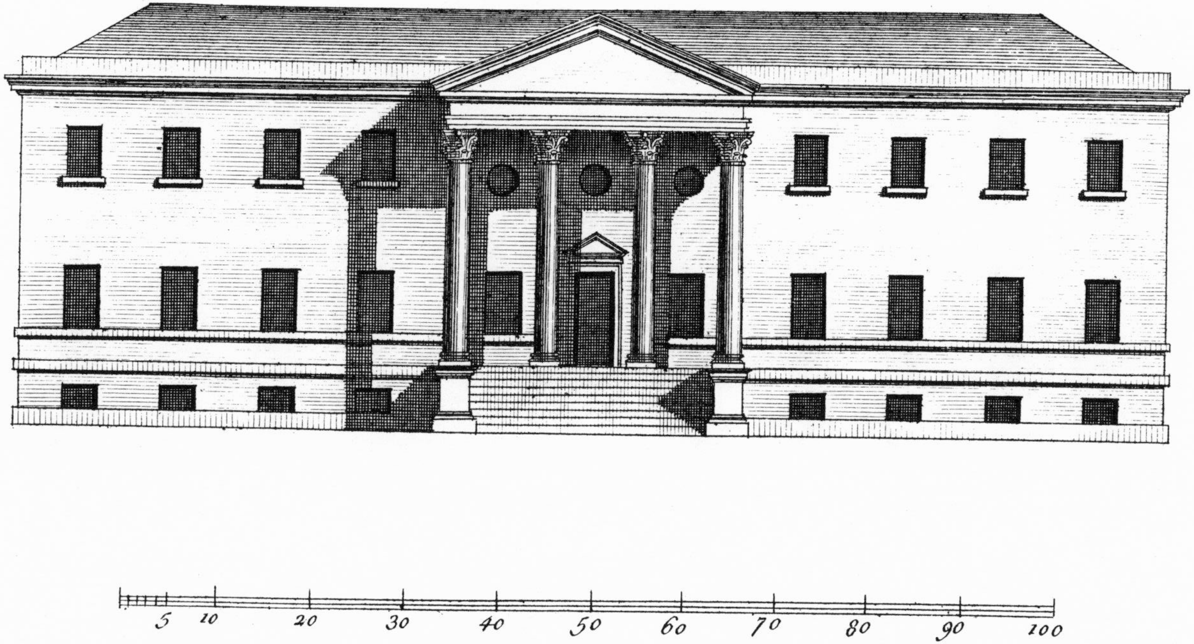

5 10   20   30   40   50   60   70   80   90   100

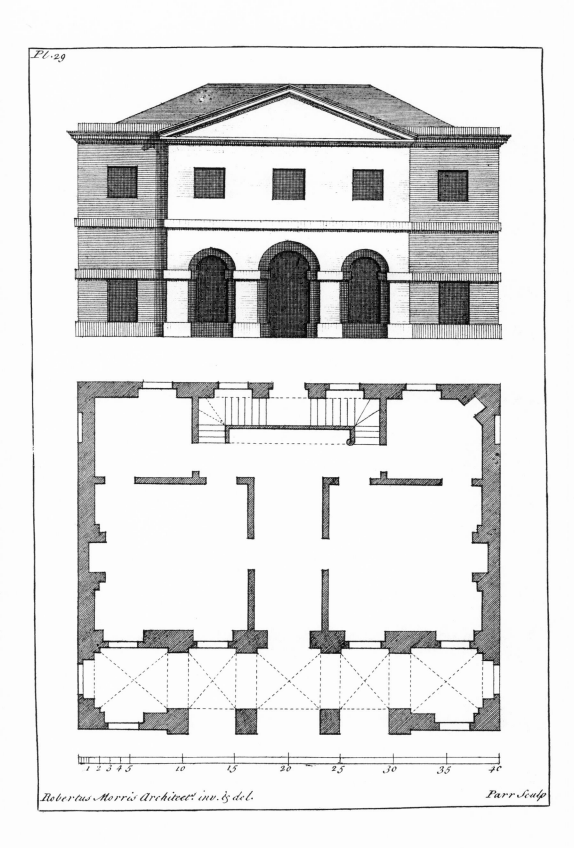

Pl. 29

1 2 3 4 5   10   15   20   25   30   35   40

Robertus Morris Architect: inv. & del.   *Parr Sculp*

Pl.30.

Rob.* Morris inv & del.

Parr Sculp

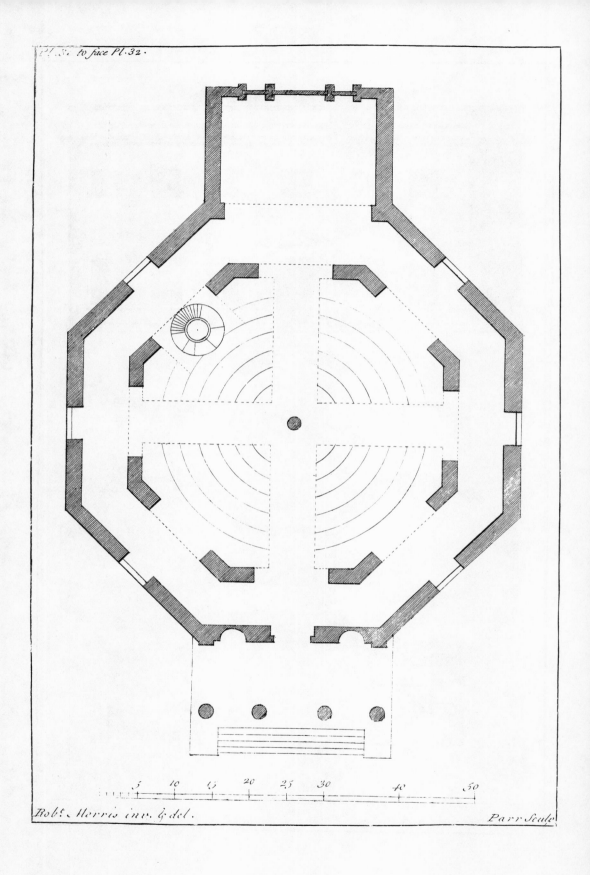

Pl. 5. to face Pl. 32.

5   10   15   20   25   30   40   50

Robt. Morris inv. & del.

Parr Scale

Pl.32.

5 10 15 20 25 30 40 50

Robt Morris inv & del.

Parr Sculp

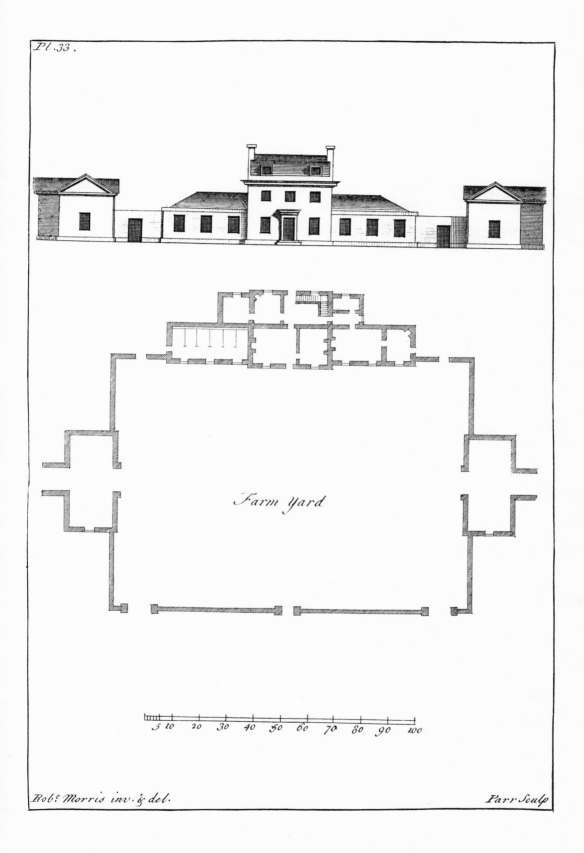

Pl. 33.

Farm Yard

5 10   20   30   40   50   60   70   80   90   100

Robᵗ Morris inv. & del.   *Parr Sculp*

Pl. 34.

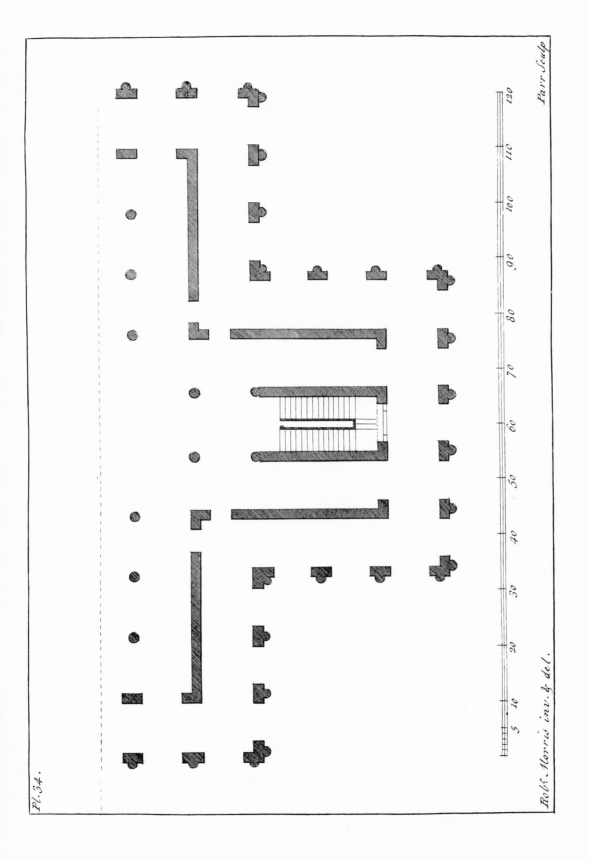

Robt. Morris inv. & del.

Parr Sculp

5 . 10   20   30   40   50   60   70   80   90   100   110   120

Pl. 35.

Rob.t Morris inv.& del.

Parr Sculp.

5 10 20 30 40 50 60 70 80 90 100 110 120

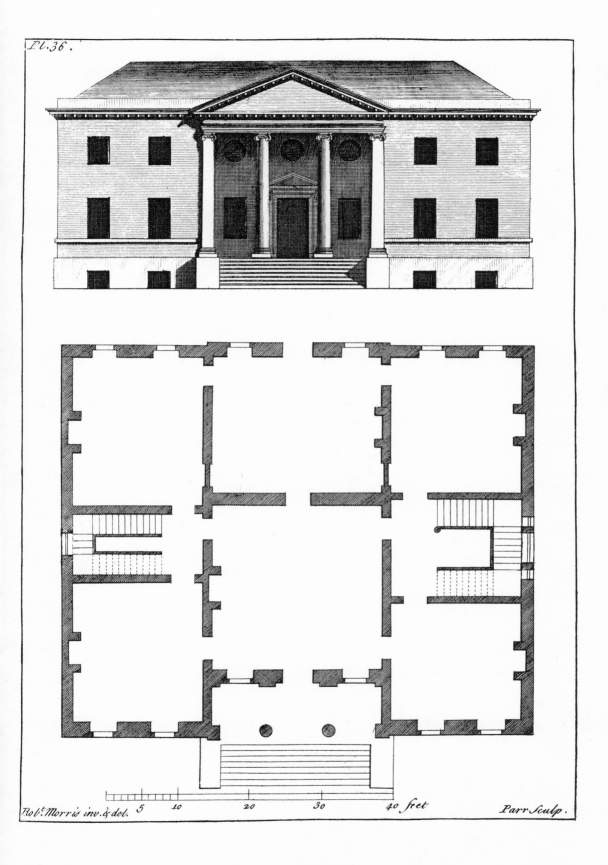

Pl. 36.

Rob.ᵗ Morris inv. & del.   5   10   20   30   40 feet   Parr Sculp.

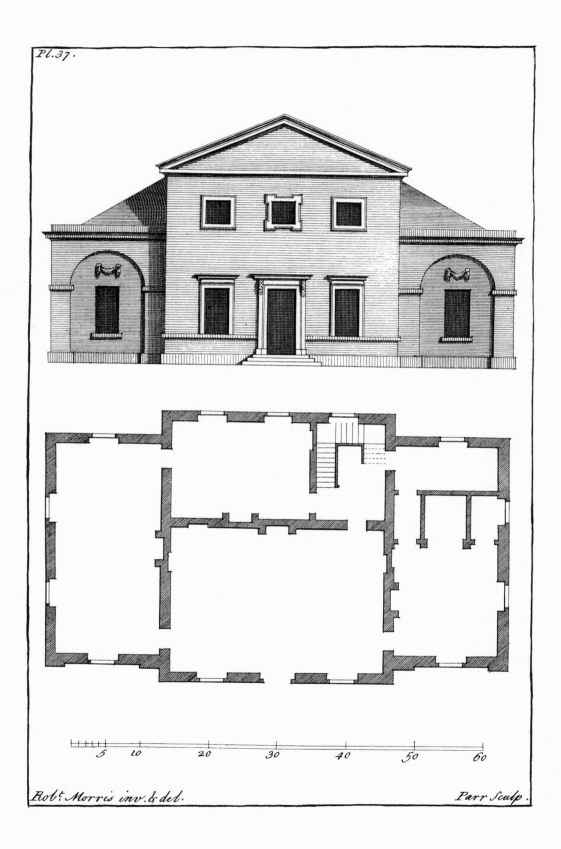

Pl. 37.

Rob.t Morris inv. & del.

Parr Sculp.

Pl.38.

C   B   A

5	10	15	20	25	30	35	40		50		60		70

Rob.t Morris inv. & del.

Parr Sculp.

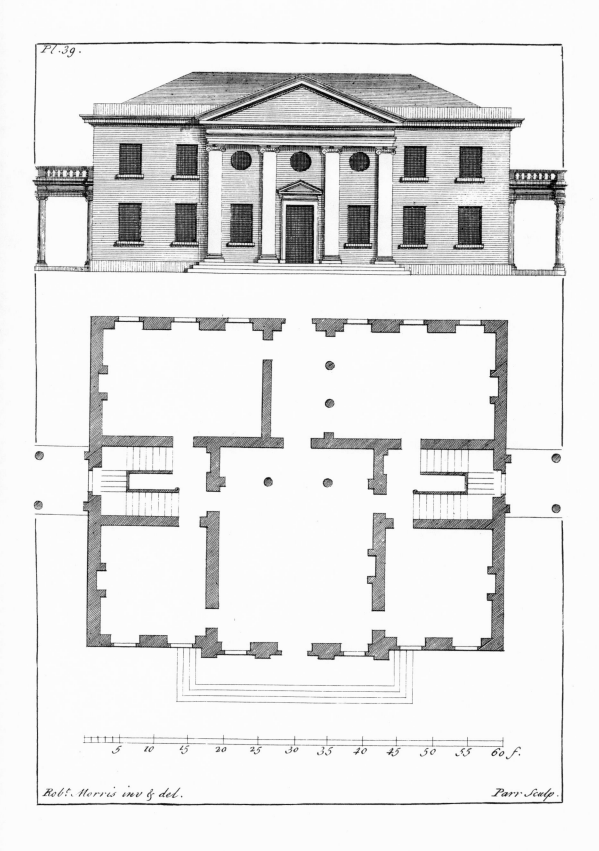

Pl. 39.

5 10 15 20 25 30 35 40 45 50 55 60 f.

Rob.t Morris inv & del.   Parr Sculp.

Pl. 40.

A
B
C

g

F

E

F

g

D

D

D

5 10 15 20 30 40 50 60 70 80 90 100

Rob.t Morris inv. & del.

Parr Sculp

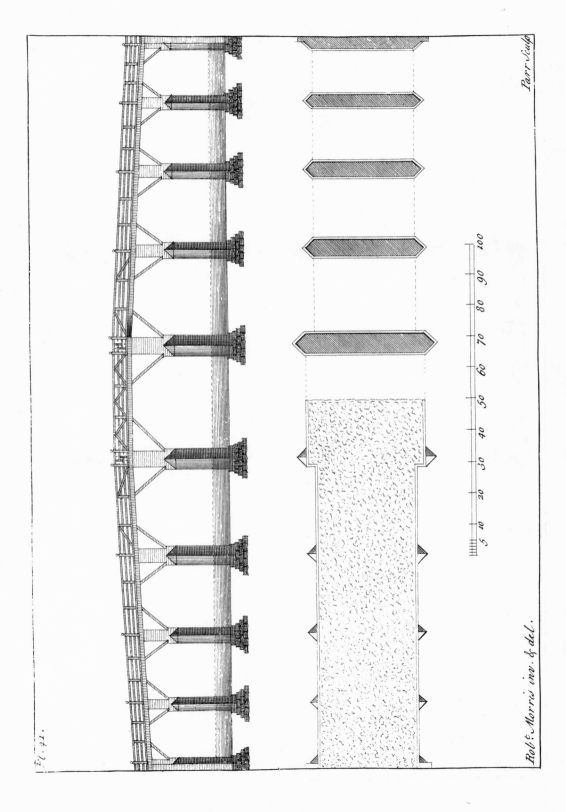

Pl. 71.

Rob.t Morris invt. & del.

Parr Sculp.

5 10 20 30 40 50 60 70 80 90 100

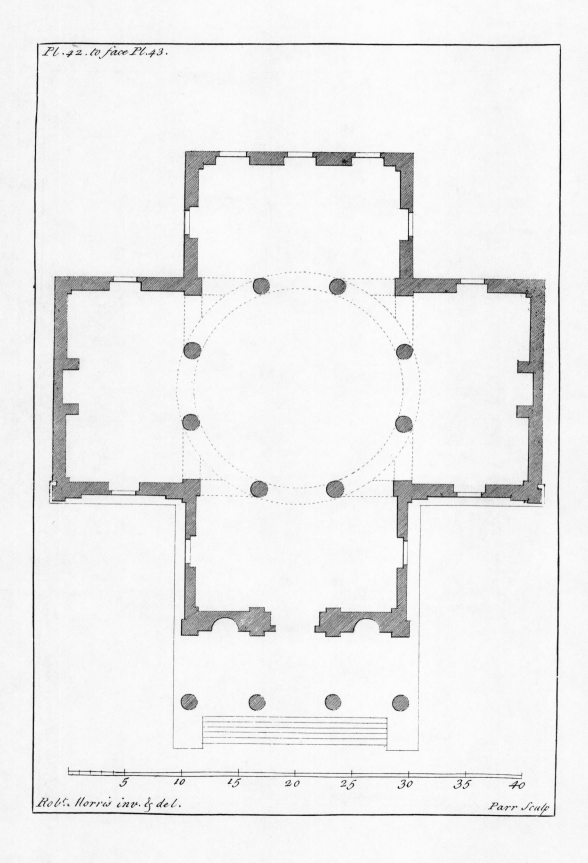

Pl. 42. to face Pl. 43.

5 10 15 20 25 30 35 40

Rob.ᵗ Morris inv. & del.

Parr Sculp

Pl. 43.

Pl. 44.

A

1 2 3 4 5   10   20   30   40   50   60

Rob.ᵗ Morris inv & del.   Parr Sculp

Pl. 45.

Robt *Morris inv. & del.*   *Parr Sculp*

Pl. 46.

Our Father

I Believe

I II III IV

V VI VII VIII IX X

1 2 3 4 5 10 15 20

Rob.t Morris inv.t & del:

Parr Sculp

Pl. 47.

A

A

5 10 15 20   30   40   50   60

Rob.t Morris inv. & del.   Parr Sculp

Pl. 48. to face Pl. 49.

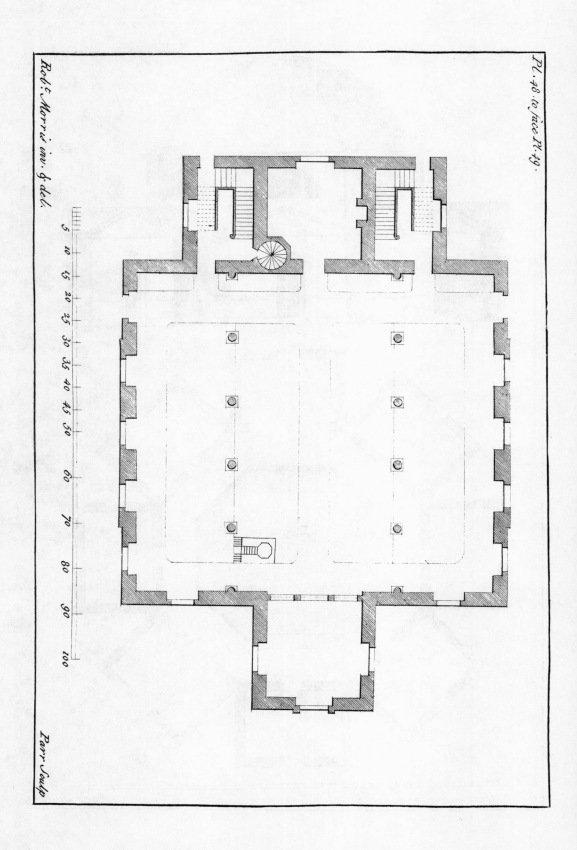

Rob.t Morris inv. & del.

Parr Sculp

5 10 15 20 25 30 35 40 45 50 60 70 80 90 100

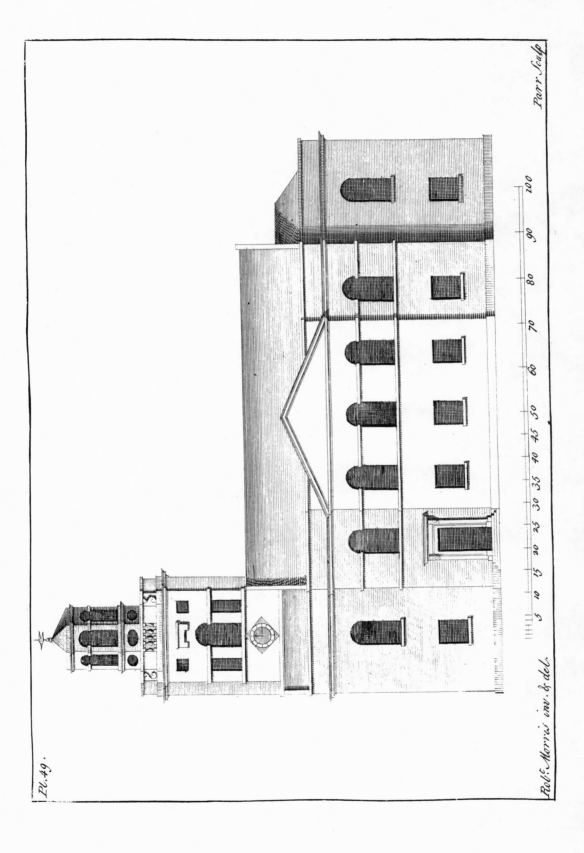

Pl. 49.

Robt. Morris inv. & del.

Parr Sculp.

Pl. 50.

5   10   15   20   25   30

Rob.t Morris inv. & del.   Parr Scalp.